Grand Diplôme Cooking Course

Volume 2

Grand Diplôme Cooking Course

A Danbury Press Book

The Danbury Press

a division of Grolier Enterprises, Inc.

Robert B. Clarke   Publisher

This book has been adapted from the Grand Diplôme Cooking Course, originally published by Purnell Cookery, U.S.A.

Purnell Grand Diplôme Editorial Board

Rosemary Hume and Muriel Downes
Principals, London Cordon Bleu Cookery
School, England

Anne Willan	Editor
Eleanor Noderer	Associate Editor
Sheryl Julian	Assistant Editor
John Paton	Managing Editor
José Northey	Co-ordinating Editor
Peter Leather	Art Editor
Charles F. Turgeon	Wine Consultant

Library of Congress Catalog Card Number: 72-13896
© B.P.C. Publishing, 1971, and
© Phoebus Publishing, 1972.
Filmsetting by Petty and Sons Ltd., Leeds, England.
Printed in the United States of America

5678998

All recipes have been tested either at the Cordon Bleu Cookery School in London or in our U.S. test kitchens.

Note: all recipe quantities in this book serve 4 people unless otherwise stated.

Contents

All recipes have been tested either at the Cordon Bleu Cookery School in London or in our U.S. test kitchens.

Note: all recipe quantities in this book serve 4 people unless otherwise stated.

From the Editor

Smooth shining sauces with subtle flavors that defy description are the essence of French cuisine. From Béchamel to demi-glace to tangy Hollandaise, the intricacies of basic sauces and their variations—Mornay, Madeira and many others—are made easy in this second volume of your Grand Diplôme Cooking Course. Just as at the London Cordon Bleu Cooking School, you can master the many ways to cook **Fish**—poach a whole salmon, sauté mackerel with garlic and tomatoes in Provençale style, bake herring in mustard sauce, stuff shad with lemon dressing, broil cod as kebabs or deep fry perch in creamy croquettes. **Frying** is an often abused technique, so don't miss the advice on fritters, French fries and fish fillets. **Roasting Meat** is equally important and here veal is discussed as thoroughly as beef, lamb and pork in Volume 1. Then graduate to greater entrées in **Roast Meats for Special Occasions** and try a contrefilet Dubarry—roast beef garnished with tiny cauliflowers—or loin of lamb Bretonne, stuffed with herbs and orange and served with an onion sauce. Less expensive meats are remembered in **Pot Roasting**, together with the **Stock** essential to a good soup or stew. Good stock also adds immeasurably to the risottos and pilafs described in **Cooking with Rice**. Perfect pastry is hard to achieve, but you'll be well on your way with the help of the instructions on **Flaky and Rough Puff Pastry** or, for a lighter dessert, it is hard to rival the delicacy of egg **Custards**, whether baked as petits pots de crème, topped with caramel as crème caramel or flavored with tangerines in a gelatin mold.

Menus are a special part of the Grand Diplôme course—they use the techniques you learn in the lessons and a timetable smooths the path from stove to table. In this volume there's a grand dinner starring duck, two meals centered on chicken and a party to please the most exacting child. At the back of the book is advice on choosing **Pots and Pans** and some points to remember when buying **Refrigerators**.

Bon Appetit!

Anne Willan

Avocado salad is served with the avocado peeled and placed rounded side up (recipe is on page 11)

MAKE A PARTY CHOICE

Don't be dismayed by the ballotine of duck stuffed with a rich mixture of ham and pistachio nuts — this classic French ballotine is easy if you follow the directions for boning given in Volume 1. Select soup or avocado salad to begin with, and for dessert there's cherry pie with a difference. All can be done with a minimum of fuss, if you follow the Timetable on page 10.

This recipe for duck demands a masculine, full-bodied red wine like a Hermitage from southeastern France. A unique alternative from America might be the new Baco Noir wine from the Finger Lakes district. This rich red is made from a French-American hybrid grape and bears no resemblance to the traditional New York State red wines.

---

*Cream of Fish Soup
or Avocado Salad*

Ballotine of Duck
Braised Celery
Boiled New Potatoes

Cherry and Praline Pie

∼∞∽

Red wine – Hermitage (Rhône)
or Baco Noir (New York)

TIMETABLE

Order of Work

Day before
Make breadcrumbs for duck.
Make sauce for duck, cover and refrigerate.
Make pastry dough for pie, put in plastic wrap and refrigerate.
Make praline for pie, and store in airtight container.

Morning
Make fish stock and cook fish for soup; *or prepare ingredients and make vinaigrette dressing for avocado and store in separate containers in a cool place.*
Prepare cherry topping for pie.
Bake pie shell. Make filling for pie, cover and keep in a cool place.
Make soup but do not add cream. Fry croûtons; keep at room temperature.
Bone duck; make stuffing for duck, stuff and sew up. Peel potatoes and cover with cold water.

Assemble equipment for final cooking from 6 p.m. for dinner around 8 p.m.

You will find that **cooking times** given in the individual recipes for these dishes have sometimes been adapted in the timetable to help you when cooking and serving them as a party meal.

6 : 00
Whip cream, add praline and filling mixture and fill pie. Spoon on topping and decorate with cherries.

6 : 15
Put duck and celery into oven, with celery on bottom shelf.

6 : 40
Baste duck and celery.

7 : 00
Turn and baste duck.

7 : 20
Baste duck and celery. Cook mushrooms.

7 : 30
Reheat soup. Cook potatoes.

7 : 45
Take duck from the roasting pan; heat sauce, turn oven to lowest setting. Put serving dishes and plates to warm. Deglaze roasting pan, add liquid and mushrooms to sauce. Add cream to soup, garnish with blanched parsley or chervil; warm croûtons in oven. *Or cut avocados, arrange on salad plates and spoon chopped ingredients and vinaigrette dressing in cavity. Garnish plate with watercress.*

7 : 50
Drain potatoes, dry and keep warm. Arrange vegetables and duck on platters and keep warm (being boned, the duck can be sliced at the table).

8 : 00
Serve appetizer.

Appetizer

Cream of Fish Soup

¾ lb fresh haddock, or flounder, fillet
3 tablespoons butter
3 tablespoons flour
¾ cup light cream
2 sprigs of parsley, or chervil (for garnish)

For stock
1 lb fish bones
1 large onion, peeled and sliced
1 tablespoon butter
1 carrot, peeled and sliced
1 stick of celery, sliced
5 cups water
bouquet garni
½ teaspoon salt
6 peppercorns
½ cup dry white wine
slice of lemon

Method
First prepare stock: thoroughly wash fish bones. Blanch onion by covering with cold water, bringing to a boil, draining and refreshing in cold water. Melt 1 tablespoon butter in a large saucepan, add onion and fish bones, cover and cook slowly for 5 minutes. Add carrot, celery, water, bouquet garni, salt, peppercorns, wine and lemon; simmer gently, uncovered, for 20 minutes. Strain stock, measure and reserve 4 cups.

Wash the fish, dry on paper towels, arrange in a saucepan or baking dish. Pour over remaining stock, cover and cook 10 minutes — in the saucepan over very low heat, or in the baking dish in a moderate oven (350°F) — or until the fish flakes easily. Flake fish, removing bones, and pound it in a mortar and pestle, or purée it in a blender with a little stock.

In a saucepan melt 3 tablespoons butter, add flour and cook gently, stirring, until straw-colored. Blend in reserved stock; stir until boiling. Simmer 5—10 minutes; whisk in the fish purée and cream. Reheat without boiling and taste for seasoning. Blanch sprigs of parsley or chervil for 1 minute in boiling water, then add to soup. Serve fried croûtons separately.

To make croûtons: cut several slices of bread into cubes, removing crusts. Fry cubes in hot shallow or deep fat until golden brown; drain on paper towels. Sprinkle lightly with salt and serve with purée and cream soups.

Alternative Appetizer

Avocado Salad

2 avocados ($\frac{1}{2}$ per person)
2 tablespoons chopped green pepper
2 tablespoons chopped green onion
6 ripe olives, pitted and chopped
watercress (for garnish)

For vinaigrette dressing
salt
black pepper, freshly ground
1$\frac{1}{2}$ tablespoons white wine vinegar
5 tablespoons oil
lemon juice (to taste)
sugar (to taste)
1 teaspoon chopped parsley

Avocado salad is an elegant appetizer. This is an alternative way of serving it to that photographed on page 8

This elegant, easy-to-prepare avocado salad makes a good appetizer, but avocados must be fully ripe to enjoy them. Test by pressing the avocado gently between the palms of your hands. If it gives and feels slightly soft, it is ripe.

Below: garnish cream of fish soup with sprigs of parsley (or chervil); serve croûtons separately

Method
Blanch chopped green pepper by boiling in water for 1 minute, draining, and rinsing in cold water.

To make dressing, mix a generous pinch of salt and black pepper with vinegar; beat in oil. Add enough lemon juice to sharpen dressing, sugar to taste, and parsley; stir in green pepper, onions and olives.

Cut avocados in half lengthwise, remove seed and brush the exposed flesh with lemon juice to prevent it from browning. Fill each cavity with dressing and chill avocados slightly before serving on individual salad plates. Garnish with watercress. Alternatively, peel avocados and serve, rounded side up, with dressing spooned over, as shown on page 8.

Ballotine of duck is served with braised celery

Entrée

Ballotine of Duck

4–5 lb duck
2 tablespoons oil
¼ lb small mushrooms, sliced
1 tablespoon butter
¼ cup sherry

For stuffing
2 tablespoons butter
1 onion, finely chopped
¾ lb pork, or veal, ground
¾ cup fresh white breadcrumbs
2 teaspoons chopped parsley
1 teaspoon sage
¼ cup sherry
¼ lb cooked ham, shredded
2 tablespoons pistachios,
    blanched and shredded
1 egg, beaten
salt and pepper

For Espagnole sauce
2 tablespoons oil
1 tablespoon finely diced
    carrots
1 tablespoon finely diced onion
½ tablespoon finely diced celery
1½ tablespoons flour
2 cups stock
few mushroom stems
¼ teaspoon tomato paste
salt and pepper
bouquet garni

*Trussing needle; fine thread,
    or string*

Method
Bone duck and set oven at hot (400°F). To prepare stuffing: melt butter in a pan, add onion and cook until soft but not colored. Combine onion with ground meat and breadcrumbs and mix well with herbs, sherry, ham and pistachio nuts. Bind mixture with beaten egg and season with salt and pepper.

Stuff duck, sew it up neatly with a trussing needle; thread and tie at intervals of 1–2 inches.

In a roasting pan heat 2 tablespoons oil, set duck on a rack in the pan and baste with hot oil. Roast duck for 1¼–1½ hours in heated oven, basting every 20 minutes and turning the bird after 40 minutes.

Meanwhile make the sauce: heat oil in a pan, add vegetables; when soft but not colored, stir in flour and cook slowly to a rich brown color. Remove pan from heat and stir in 1 cup stock and remaining sauce ingredients. Return to heat, stir until sauce boils, and simmer very gently, with lid half on, for 20–30 minutes. Add half remaining cold stock, skim sauce well and simmer 5 minutes longer. Add the rest of the stock, skim sauce again and simmer another 5 minutes. Strain.

Cook sliced mushrooms in 1 tablespoon butter until soft. Remove duck from roasting pan, pour off fat and deglaze with sherry. Strain and add to sauce with cooked mushrooms.

Serve the duck whole or sliced, pour over a little sauce and serve the rest separately.

Since duck is a rich meat, serve boiled potatoes with it, preferably little new ones. Braised celery is a good second vegetable.

> **To deglaze:** after removing excess fat, to heat stock and/or wine together with sediments left in roasting/frying pan so that gravy/sauce is formed.

> **A ballotine** refers to a piece of meat, poultry, game or fish that is boned, stuffed and rolled into the shape of a bundle — a 'ballot'. It is tied with string at intervals to keep its shape, or secured with skewers, or poultry pins. A ballotine is always served hot.

Accompaniments to Entrée

Boiled New Potatoes

New potatoes are an exception to the rule that the boiling of root vegetables should be started in cold water.

Choose the smallest potatoes possible, of an even size. Wash them and scrub with a pot scrubber or small brush; this should be sufficient to remove the skin; if not, use a vegetable peeler. Put the potatoes in a large pan of boiling salted water and cook for 15–20 minutes, according to size, or until they are just tender when pierced with the point of a knife, or with a skewer — they should remain firm and waxy in texture. Drain and toss with melted butter.

A little chopped mint is an excellent addition to new potatoes if they are to be served with plain roast or broiled meat.

Braised Celery

bunch of celery
1 large onion, diced
1 large carrot, diced
2 tablespoons butter
½ cup jellied stock (see page 18)
salt and pepper
bouquet garni

Method
Wash celery and slice off some of the leaves. Split the bunch in four and blanch in boiling salted water; drain.

In a large flameproof casserole sweat onion and carrot in butter by covering tightly with foil and the lid and cooking over very low heat until vegetables are soft but not brown.

Put celery, stock, salt, pepper and the bouquet garni in with the vegetables. Cover and braise for 1–1½ hours or until tender in a moderately low oven (325°F), basting from time to time. When cooked, the sauce should be well reduced and the celery glazed. Strain sauce and pour over celery in a vegetable dish.

Dessert

Cherry and Praline Pie

For French pie pastry
1¼ cups flour
pinch of salt
6 tablespoons butter, softened
6 tablespoons sugar
3 egg yolks
½ teaspoon vanilla extract

For praline filling
¼ cup unblanched almonds
6½ tablespoons sugar
1 cup milk
1 egg
2 teaspoons cornstarch
pinch of salt
½ cup heavy cream, whipped

For topping
1 can dark dessert cherries, pitted
½ cup red wine
3–4 tablespoons red currant jelly
grated rind of 1 orange

9 inch pie pan

Method

First prepare pastry dough: sift flour with salt onto a board or marble slab and make a large well in center. Into this put butter, sugar, egg yolks and vanilla; work together with the fingertips until smooth. Gradually draw in flour; work with hand to form a smooth dough. Chill 1 hour, roll out and line pie pan. If pastry is too stiff to roll, leave at room temperature to soften for 5–10 minutes before rolling. Bake blind 15–20 minutes in a moderately hot oven (375°F) or until pie shell is lightly browned.

To make filling: in a small heavy pan or skillet, heat almonds and 4 tablespoons sugar together until sugar is liquid caramel. Stir it care-fully with a metal spoon to toast almonds on all sides. When dark brown pour mixture into an oiled pan to cool and solidify. When firm, remove from pan and crush with a rolling pin, or work praline through a rotary cheese grater, or grinder, or pound with a rolling pin. Set aside.

Heat 1 cup milk in a small saucepan until a skin forms on top. In a bowl combine the egg, 2 tablespoons sugar, cornstarch and salt. Pour in hot milk very gradually, stirring constantly. Return mixture to saucepan; cook over low heat, stirring constantly, until it begins to thicken. Pour into bowl and cover with wax paper to prevent a skin from forming.

To prepare topping: drain cherries thoroughly. Cook wine to reduce it to 2 tablespoons, add red currant jelly and orange rind and heat gently until jelly is melted. Stir in cherries (reserve a few for garnish) and cool the mixture. Fold whipped cream, sweetened with the remaining sugar, into cold filling mixture with ¼ cup praline. Taste, add more sugar if needed. Fill cool pie shell with praline cream. Spoon on cherry topping and garnish with reserved cherries.

Grating the caramelized sugar and almonds for praline

For French flan pastry, put the sugar, egg yolks, butter and vanilla into the well in the center of the flour

With your fingertips, work the ingredients to a paste

Draw in the flour quickly, using a metal spatula, and work with the whole hand to form a smooth dough. Chill

---

Praline is a mixture of almonds and caramelized sugar which is usually ground or crushed before being added to desserts such as this cherry and praline pie, soufflés, creams, ice creams, etc. Praline is often used in confectionery, e.g. mixed with chocolate for rich fillings.

The origin of the name (for a sugared almond) dates from the time of Louis XIII. The Duc de Choiseul-Praslin was re-nowned for his conquests both in battle and in the bedroom. He once offered his favorite mistress a new confection (a sugared almond, in fact) which had such success that it was called prasline, and a confectionery shop was opened especially to sell it.

Serve rich cherry and praline pie as an unusual cold dessert for a dinner party

ḣOW TO

Ingredients for general purpose ordinary stock, that is used for making gravies and simple soups and sauces

MAKE STOCK

The French call stock 'fonds de cuisine' and it is literally the basis for the preparation of soups, sauces, and gravies. Stock is easy to make, the ingredients are not expensive, and the best casseroles, stews, braises and sauces owe their fine flavor to the stock that is added during cooking. Poor stock can turn a promising dish into a tasteless mixture so, if you want to try a recipe which needs good stock and none is available, *change your choice of dish.* You will only be disappointed if you try to compromise.

Most kitchens have the vegetables, carcass bones, etc., to make simple stock for a gravy or a quick sauce. For larger quantities, a few beef bones will make enough stock to last most cooks a week. Bones alone give a stronger stock than if vegetables and meat are combined, and the older and more mature the ingredients, the more flavor the stock will have. In fact, stock-making is an exception to almost every other kind of cooking in that it doesn't call for things young and tender.

Raw lamb bones and turnips are best omitted from stock unless it is intended for Scotch broth; both have a strong flavor which may easily spoil the dish to which the stock is added. It is also wise to use strong-flavored herbs very sparingly because the flavor of the stock will be highly concentrated at the end of reduction.

When cooked, stock should be reduced in quantity by simmering over a steady low heat, by at least one quarter before it is strained. Stock may be kept 2 weeks or more in the refrigerator if, every 3–4 days it is brought to a boil and simmered 10 minutes. Before using, lift off any fat which has solidified on the surface. Strained stock, with the fat removed, may also be frozen.

In an emergency, canned or powdered bouillon may be used for certain dishes, but it can never replace homemade stock as it lacks the characteristic jellied quality. Commercial bouillon contains salt so beware of adding too much seasoning. If you often substitute bouillon for homemade stock, your dishes will have a monotonous flavor.

Mixed Stock

The only way to make really clear stock is with raw bones, but if you use cooked ones as well it helps to add these after the stock has come to a boil. If the stock is to be kept for any length of time it is better not to mix raw and cooked bones.

Any leftovers of meat can be added to a stock pot: chicken carcasses and giblets (not the liver), meat bones and trimmings from steak (provided they are not too fatty), or a ham bone (which makes an excellent stock for pea or bean soup).

Add a plateful of coarsely chopped root vegetables, bouquet garni, 5–6 peppercorns and enough cold water, up to about two-thirds above level of ingredients. Season with a little salt (none if a ham bone has been added). Bring slowly to a boil, skim, half cover the pan and simmer $1\frac{1}{2}$–2 hours or longer, depending on the quantity of stock being made. The liquid should reduce by about one third. Strain and, when the stock is cold, skim off any fat. Discard the ingredients unless a fair amount of raw bone has been used, in which case more water may be added and a second boiling done.

Watchpoint: long, slow simmering is essential for any meat stock. It should never be allowed to boil hard as this will result in a thick muddy-looking jellied stock instead of a clear one.

Brown Bone Stock

3 lb beef bones, or mixed
   beef/veal bones
2 onions, quartered
2 carrots, quartered
1 stalk of celery, cut in 4 pieces
large bouquet garni
6 peppercorns
2 teaspoons salt
3–4 quarts water

Large saucepan, or kettle (6 quart capacity)

Method
Wipe the bones, but do not wash them unless necessary as they will brown better if not washed. Put into a very large pan over gentle heat and leave to fry gently for 15–20 minutes or until golden brown, turning occasionally. Fat will be released from the marrow, so do not add any to pan unless bones are very dry.

After 10 minutes, add vegetables and brown. Add bouquet garni, peppercorns, salt and water, up to two-thirds above the level of ingredients. Bring slowly to a boil, skimming occasionally, then half cover the pan so the stock can reduce. Simmer 4–5 hours or until it tastes strong and good.

Strain the stock and use the

bones again for a second boiling. This second stock will not be as strong as the first, but it is good for soups and gravies. Use the first stock for brown sauces, sautés, casseroles, or when a jellied stock is required. For a strong beef stock, add 1 lb shank of beef to the pan halfway through cooking.

Bouquet garni is a bunch of herbs traditionally made of 2–3 parsley stalks, a sprig of fresh thyme (or a pinch of dried thyme) and a bay leaf (tied together with string if used in liquids which are to be strained). Otherwise tie herbs in a piece of cheesecloth for easy removal before serving.

Ingredients for white bone (veal bones only) stock, that forms a basis for cream sauces

White Bone Stock

This stock forms the basis of cream sauces, white stews, etc. It is made in the same way as brown bone stock, except that bones and vegetables are not browned before the water is added and veal bones only are used. Do not add vegetables until the bones have come to a boil and the fat has been skimmed from the liquid.

Vegetable Stock

6 carrots, quartered
4 medium onions, quartered
5 stalks of celery, quartered
1 tablespoon butter
3–4 peppercorns
1 teaspoon tomato purée
2½ quarts water
1 teaspoon salt

Method
In a large pan or kettle, brown vegetables in butter. Add remaining ingredients, bring to a boil, cover pan and simmer 2 hours or until the stock has good flavor. Strain and store in the refrigerator.

Chicken or Duck Stock

giblets of bird (neck, gizzard, heart and feet, if available)
oil (for frying)
1 onion, halved and washed but not peeled
1 quart cold water
¼ teaspoon salt
a few peppercorns
bouquet garni

Never add the liver when making chicken or duck stock as it gives a bitter flavor; it is best used for making pâté or sautéed for a snack.

Method
Heat a heavy saucepan with enough oil almost to cover the base; then add the giblets and onion and fry over a high heat until lightly browned. Remove the pan from the heat and add the water, salt, peppercorns and bouquet garni. Cover and simmer gently for 1–2 hours. Strain before use.

Fish Stock

1–1½ lb fish bones, washed
1 large onion, peeled and sliced
1 tablespoon butter
1 carrot, peeled and sliced
1 stalk of celery, sliced
5 cups water
bouquet garni
½ teaspoon salt
6 peppercorns
½ cup dry white wine
slice of lemon

Method
Blanch the onion by placing in a pan of cold water, bringing to a boil, draining, refreshing in cold water, and draining again.

Melt the butter in a large saucepan, add the onion and fish bones, cover and cook slowly for 5 minutes. Add the remaining ingredients and simmer gently, uncovered, for 20 minutes; strain and measure.

Note: in a future Volume recipes for making consommé and clear broth will be given.

Fowl-in-the-pot, surrounded by sliced vegetables, is ready for pot roasting (recipe is on page 22)

HOW TO POT ROAST

Pot roasting is one of the best and easiest ways to deal with the cheaper cuts of meat that need slow cooking to prevent them from becoming dry and tasteless. Poultry is excellent pot roasted; not only older fowls but also roasting birds and small broiling chickens keep all their flavor and succulence when cooked in this way. As an added advantage, the meat needs a minimum of attention once it has started to cook.

The only essential for pot roasting is the right type of flameproof casserole — thick iron, enameled iron or aluminum — with a close-fitting lid, deep and big enough to hold a cut of meat or a bird comfortably.

The procedure is simple: the meat or bird is browned all over; root vegetables and a bouquet garni are added but no liquid unless stated in the recipe. Even then it should not measure more than $\frac{1}{2}$ cup, usually of stock or wine. Add a little salt and pepper, close lid tightly and set on a low heat or, if more convenient, in a low oven. The cooking time depends on the size of the bird or cut of meat and is given in each recipe.

Meat is served like a roast, with accompanying vegetables cooked separately; those done with the meat will be overcooked and have little flavor. The flavor is in the gravy; this is strained, well-skimmed of fat and may be diluted with stock.

Pot roasted meat or chicken can be served in different ways, varied by sauces and garnishes.

21

Fowl-in-the-pot

4–5 lb fowl
1–2 tablespoons butter, or
    meat drippings
3 slices of bacon
1 onion, sliced
1 carrot, sliced
1 stalk of celery, sliced
bouquet garni
salt and pepper
2 teaspoons flour (for gravy)

For garnish
chipolata, or country, sausages
bacon rolls

Trussing needle and string, or
skewers

Method
Truss the fowl or secure with skewers. In a deep flame-proof casserole, or Dutch oven, brown the bird carefully all over in butter or drippings. Remove from pot and pour off all the fat (there is a good deal in a fowl). Lay bacon slices in bottom of pot, set bird on them and surround it with the prepared vegetables. Add bouquet garni and season lightly.

Cover with foil and lid and cook over very low heat or in a moderately low oven (325°F) for about $2\frac{1}{2}$ hours, depending on the size of the bird or until the thigh is very tender and no pink juice runs out when pierced with a fork or skewer. Take fowl from the pot, set on a platter and keep warm.

Strain juice from the pot, skimming off fat, and mix 2 teaspoons of this fat with the flour. Stir into the juice, dilute with a little chicken stock, or water, to taste and bring to a boil, stirring. Simmer 5 minutes to cook flour.

To make garnish: cut each strip of bacon in half, roll and impale these on a skewer. Broil bacon with sausages

until crisp and brown and arrange them around fowl. Spoon over a little gravy and serve the rest separately. If you like, the bird may be carved in the kitchen and served, covered, in a shallow casserole.

Pot Roast Chicken

2 broiling chickens ($1\frac{1}{2}$–2 lb each)
3 tablespoons butter
salt and pepper
juice of $\frac{1}{2}$ lemon
little stock (made from the giblets), or wine
1 tablespoon kneaded butter

Trussing needle and string, or
skewers

Method
Truss the chickens or secure with skewers. In a deep flame-proof casserole, melt butter and brown birds slowly on all sides. Place them on their backs, add seasoning and sprinkle with lemon juice. Cover pot and cook over a low heat for 30 minutes or until birds are very tender. Split the birds in half and arrange on a platter.

Deglaze the pot with a little stock or wine. Thicken this gravy with kneaded butter and spoon it over the birds. Serve with a salad or cooked vegetable.

The giblets (without the liver) should be made into a small quantity of stock for the gravy.

Note: see deglazing instructions on page 13.

Pot Roast Pheasant

5 lb pheasant, or other game bird
thinly sliced pork fat, or bacon (for barding)
2 tablespoons butter
1 onion, quartered
1 carrot, quartered
bouquet garni
$\frac{3}{4}$–1 cup chicken stock
$\frac{1}{4}$ cup sherry (optional)

Trussing needle and string, or
skewers

Pot roasting is a good way to cook game like pheasant, or older birds which tend to be tough and dry when roasted.

Method
Truss the bird or secure with skewers. Cover breast of bird with pork fat or bacon. In a deep flameproof casserole heat butter on top of stove and, when foaming, add pheasant. Surround with vegetables and add bouquet garni. Season very lightly. Cover and cook 5–6 minutes over a medium heat until vegetables begin to color and steam starts to rise.

Reduce heat and simmer gently for $1\frac{1}{2}$ hours, or until the bird is tender and no pink juice runs out when pierced in the thigh with a fork or skewer.

Take out pheasant, remove the barding fat or bacon, arrange bird on a platter and keep hot. Remove bouquet garni, deglaze pan with the stock and add the sherry if liked. Season, strain and serve separately as a gravy.

Alternatively, the pheasant may be carved and arranged on a platter with the gravy spooned over top and vegetables such as braised cabbage, or celery, served separately.

Pot Roast Shoulder of Lamb

1 small shoulder of lamb, boned but not rolled
1 tablespoon oil, or meat drippings
2 medium onions, sliced
1–2 sticks of celery, or 1 turnip, sliced
2 carrots, sliced
2 tablespoons kneaded butter, or little arrowroot, or corn-starch

For stuffing
$\frac{1}{2}$ lb pork sausage meat
1 tablespoon oil, or meat drippings
1 medium onion, finely chopped
1–2 parsley stalks, chopped
1 tablespoon mixed chopped herbs (thyme, marjoram, basil, oregano)
1 clove of garlic, crushed (optional)
salt and pepper

Trussing needle and string, or
skewers

Method
First prepare the stuffing: in a frying pan or skillet, heat oil, add onion and fry until soft. Add to sausage meat with herbs, garlic and seasoning. Fill into the lamb and sew up or fasten with skewers and string. In a large flameproof casserole, brown meat in oil or drippings and remove from pot. Then brown onions, celery or turnip and carrots in pot. Drain off any excess fat, put back the lamb and cover the pot tightly.

Cook very slowly on top of the stove or in a moderately low oven (325°F) for $2\frac{1}{2}$ hours or until meat is very tender. Take out lamb, arrange it on a platter, remove string or skewers and keep warm. Strain juice from pan, skimming off the fat. Add a little extra stock to the juice if necessary and thicken lightly with kneaded butter, or a little arrowroot or cornstarch. Serve lamb with vegetables of your choice cooked separately.

Pot Roast Leg of Lamb Provençale

5–6 lb leg of lamb
2 cloves of garlic, cut in slivers
6 anchovy fillets, cut in 1 inch lengths
2 tablespoons olive oil
1 onion, sliced
½ cup stock
salt and pepper

For sauce
3 shallots or scallions, finely chopped
1 tablespoon butter
1 tablespoon flour
2 anchovy fillets, finely chopped
2 gherkin pickles, finely chopped
2 teaspoons tomato paste
1 cup stock (made from the shank bone of the lamb)

For garnish
4 medium tomatoes, peeled and halved
1 tablespoon butter
2 teaspoons chopped parsley
2 anchovy fillets, cut in half lengthwise

Larding needle

Innumerable dishes are described as in the style of Provence. This simply means that they are cooked or garnished with ingredients that are popular there – often this is garlic and tomatoes but anchovies, olives and herbs like thyme, basil, oregano and fennel are also typical.

Pot roast leg of lamb provençale is garnished with tomato halves decorated with strips of anchovy fillet and hot parsley butter poured over them

Method
Make slits with the point of a knife near the bone of the lamb and insert the garlic slivers. Lard the surface of the meat with the 1 inch strips of anchovy.

In a deep flameproof casserole heat the oil and brown the lamb on all sides. Take out, add the onion and brown also. Drain off any excess fat.

Replace the lamb and add the stock and seasoning. Cover and cook very slowly on top of the stove, turning the meat from time to time, or cook in a moderately low oven (325°F) for 2½–3 hours or until the lamb is tender when pierced with a skewer. During the last 5 minutes cooking,

add the tomatoes for garnish, so they heat thoroughly.

To make the sauce: cook the shallots or scallions in the butter until lightly browned, stir in the flour and add the chopped anchovy fillets, gherkin pickles, tomato paste and stock. Bring to a boil, stirring, and simmer 4–5 minutes.

To prepare the garnish: melt 1 tablespoon butter in a pan and stir in the parsley. Transfer the lamb to a platter, arrange the tomatoes around it and cross 2 strips of anchovy on top of each tomato half; spoon over the parsley butter and keep warm.

Strain the cooking liquid from the casserole into the sauce, skim off any fat and

taste for seasoning – it should be quite spicy. Serve the sauce separately, with boulangère potatoes (see Volume 1) as an accompaniment.

Pot Roast Pork Marielle

3 lb pork loin, boned and
  rolled
1 tablespoon oil
1 tablespoon butter
1 medium onion, chopped
2 cups jellied stock
bouquet garni
1 teaspoon chopped tarragon,
  or oregano

Method

In a deep flameproof cas-
serole, heat oil and butter
and brown pork on all sides.
Remove, add onion and brown.
Drain off any excess fat and
replace meat in pot, add 1
cup stock with bouquet garni
and tarragon or oregano,
and simmer, uncovered, over
very low heat until the stock
is reduced to a few tablespoons. Add $\frac{1}{2}$ cup more
stock and repeat reducing
process. Add remaining stock,
cover pot with foil and lid and
cook over a very low heat or
in a moderately low oven
(325°F) for about 3 hours or
until pork is very tender.

Take out the meat, slice it
and arrange on a platter.
Strain the liquid from the pot,
spoon a little over the meat
and serve the rest separately.

To serve cold, allow pork
and strained liquid to cool.
Chill liquid until set to a jellied consistency and chop it.
Slice pork, arrange on a platter and garnish with chopped
jellied liquid.

Beef Pot Roast

3 lb shoulder, or chuck roast,
  of beef, boned and rolled
1 tablespoon oil, or meat
  drippings
1 onion, stuck with 1 clove
1 carrot, sliced
bouquet garni
$\frac{1}{2}$ cup red wine, or stock
salt
black pepper, freshly ground
2 teaspoons flour (for gravy)

Method

Heat oil or drippings in a
deep flameproof casserole
until very hot. Add meat and
brown it on all sides. Remove,
pouring off any surplus fat;
leave 1 tablespoon of fat in
the bottom of the pot. Replace meat and tuck the prepared vegetables down the
sides with the bouquet garni.

Pour over wine or stock and
season very lightly. Lay a
piece of foil or buttered paper
over beef so that the cover
fits tightly and there is no
danger of the meat becoming
hard from contact with the lid
while cooking. Cook over a
low heat or, if liked, in a
moderately low oven (325°F),
for about 3 hours or until
meat is tender when pierced
with a fork or skewer. Turn
it once or twice if cooking on
top of the stove.

Remove beef, set on a
platter and keep warm. Make
the gravy as for fowl-in-the-
pot (see page 22).

Slice beef and arrange on
platter. Spoon over the gravy
and garnish with vegetables
of your choice.

Pot Roast Beef Diabolo

3–4 lb beef arm, or blade roast
3 tablespoons oil, or meat
  drippings
$\frac{1}{4}$ cup finely chopped onion
$\frac{1}{2}$ cup stock
salt and pepper
2 tablespoons prepared
  mustard
$\frac{1}{4}$ cup chili sauce
1 tablespoon Worcestershire
  sauce
1 tablespoon vinegar
1 tablespoon sugar
2 tablespoons flour
$\frac{1}{4}$ cup water

Method

In a deep flameproof cas-
serole, heat oil or drippings
and brown meat on all sides.
Pour off excess fat, leaving 1
tablespoon, and add onion
and half the stock. Season
lightly, cover pot tightly and
cook over a low heat on top
of stove or in a moderately
low oven (325°F) for $2\frac{1}{2}$
hours.

Combine the mustard, chili
sauce, Worcestershire sauce,
vinegar, sugar and flour and
stir in the water. Pour this
over the meat and continue
cooking 30 minutes or until
meat is very tender. Transfer
meat to a platter and add
remaining stock to the pot.
Simmer 5 minutes, strain,
and spoon a little of this sauce
over the beef, serving the rest
separately.

Accompany this hot beef
dish with cooked root vegetables, or serve cold with
potato salad and sliced beets.

New Orleans Pot Roast Beef

4 lb round, or chuck, roast of
  beef
12 large pimiento-stuffed
  olives
$\frac{3}{4}$ lb salt pork, diced
2 large onions, chopped
$\frac{1}{2}$ cup rum
4 tomatoes, peeled, seeded
  and chopped, or 2 cups
  canned tomatoes
bouquet garni
$\frac{1}{2}$ teaspoon chopped basil
2 cloves of garlic, crushed
black pepper, freshly ground
sprig of mint (for garnish)

Method

Make a double row of slits in
beef on each side and insert
the olives, halved lengthwise.
Tie meat into a roll with string
at 2 inch intervals.

In a large, deep flameproof
casserole cook pork on top of
stove, stirring occasionally,
until brown. Remove, add
beef and brown on all sides.
Drain off excess fat, leaving
1 tablespoon, and in this
brown the onion. Replace
beef and pork, add rum and
flame it by igniting it in the
pot over medium heat.

Watchpoint: stand back, as
the flames may rise quite
high. Extinguish them after
1 minute by covering the pot
with the lid. Add tomatoes,
bouquet garni, basil, garlic,
and pepper to taste. Cover
and cook over very low heat
or in a low oven (300°F)
for 4–5 hours or until beef is
tender enough to cut with a
spoon. If the pot becomes dry
during cooking, add a little
stock. Transfer beef to a
platter, garnish with mint,
spoon over the sauce after
removing bouquet garni and
serve.

New Orleans pot roast beef is garnished with a sprig of mint

HOW TO MAKE PASTRY (2)
Flaky and Rough Puff

Both flaky and rough puff pastry originated in farmhouse kitchens where lard from home-butchered pigs and homemade butter were readily available. These pastries are richer and more flaky than regular pie pastry and are very popular crusts for sweet and savory pies, as well as forming the basis for many of the English regional specialties like Norfolk apple dumplings.

Flaky Pastry

2 cups flour
pinch of salt
6 tablespoons butter
6 tablespoons shortening,
    or lard
8–10 tablespoons ice water

Method

Sift flour with salt into a bowl. Divide fats into four portions (two of butter, two of shortening or lard and use alternatively); rub one portion, butter or shortening, with the fingertips into the flour and mix with enough cold water to make a firm dough. The amount of water varies with different flours, but an average quantity for 2 cups flour is just over $\frac{1}{2}$ cup or 8–10 tablespoons. The more finely ground the flour, the more water it will absorb.

Knead dough lightly until smooth, then roll out to a rectangle about 6 X 15 inches. Put a second portion of fat (not the same kind as the first portion rubbed in), cut in small pieces, onto two-thirds of the dough. Fold in three, put in a cloth or plastic wrap and chill 15 minutes. Place dough so open edge is towards you, roll out to a rectangle. Put on a third portion of fat in pieces, fold dough in three, put in a cloth or plastic wrap and refrigerate 15 minutes.

Roll out dough again, put on remaining fat, cut in pieces, roll and fold as before. If dough is streaky, give one more turn and roll out and fold. If wrapped in an airtight plastic bag, dough keeps up to 1 week in refrigerator, or for several weeks in the freezer.

For flaky pastry: mixing fat and flour to a firm dough

Above: folding rectangle of dough spread with a second portion of fat cut in pieces

Below: rolling out the dough before spreading rest of fat

Rough Puff Pastry 1

2 cups flour
pinch of salt
$\frac{3}{4}$ cup best quality butter
    or margarine
10 tablespoons ice water

This recipe is quicker to make than the second one, although the same ingredients are used in both methods. You can use either type, but the second is likely to be a little lighter.

Method

Sift flour with salt into a bowl. Cut butter or margarine in even pieces about the size of a walnut and drop into the flour. Mix quickly with water to prevent dough from becoming starchy with overworking and turn onto a lightly floured board.

Complete the following action (called a 'turn') three times: roll dough into a rectangle, about 6 X 15 inches, fold in thirds (like a business letter) and make a half-turn to bring the open edges facing you. Roll out again and repeat process. After three rollings or 'turns' chill pastry 15 minutes. Give an extra roll and fold if it looks streaky. Chill, or freeze, as for flaky pastry.

Roll out and use as required.

Rough Puff Pastry 2

2 cups flour
pinch of salt
$\frac{3}{4}$ cup best quality butter
    or margarine
10 tablespoons ice water

Method

Sift flour with salt into a bowl. Rub 2 tablespoons butter or margarine into the flour and mix to a firm but pliable dough with the water. Knead lightly until smooth and chill 10–15 minutes.

Place remaining butter between 2 sheets of wax paper and beat to a flat pliable cake with a rolling pin. The butter should be the same consistency as the dough.

Roll out dough into a rectangle, about 6 X 15 inches, place butter cake in the middle, fold dough over butter like a parcel, seal edges, turn over.

Complete the following action (called a 'turn') three times: roll out dough to a rectangle, about 6 X 15 inches, fold in thirds and make a half-turn to bring the open edge towards you. After three rollings or 'turns', chill or freeze as for flaky pastry. Roll out and use as required.

In a hot kitchen: the fat may break through the dough and start sticking to the board during rolling. When this happens, complete the rolling as fast as possible, dust dough lightly with flour on both sides, put it in plastic wrap and chill it until firm and easy to handle. In fact, it is a good idea to chill flaky and rough puff pastry for 15 minutes between each rolling and 'turn'.

Be sure to clean pastry board between rollings as any bits left on the board will stick to the dough and make it lumpy.

Quantity Terms
Terms like **'2 cup quantity of pastry'** refer to the amount of dough obtained by using 2 cups of flour, *not 2 cups of prepared pastry dough*. As a quantity guide, 2 cup quantity of flaky, or rough puff, pastry will line two 9 inch pie pans, or are enough for a double crust 9 inch pie.

Flaky Pastry

Veal and Ham Pie

2 cup quantity of flaky pastry, well chilled
1½ lb veal shoulder
¼ lb cooked lean ham, cut in strips
1 tablespoon finely chopped onion
2 teaspoons finely chopped parsley
1 teaspoon grated lemon rind
salt and pepper
3 hard-cooked eggs, quartered
2 cups jellied stock, well seasoned
1 egg, beaten to mix

Deep 9 inch pie dish

Veal and ham pie is one of the most popular traditional dishes in England. Substantial wedges are sold at sports stadiums and race tracks throughout the country, and a pint of beer and a piece of pie make a popular snack at the local pub.

Method
Cut veal in 1–1½ inch cubes. Mix onion, parsley, lemon rind, salt and pepper together and roll meat in this mixture. Arrange veal, ham and eggs in layers until dish is full, doming top slightly, and pour in enough stock to fill dish three quarters full. Set oven at hot (425°F).

Roll out pastry dough into a circle, cut a strip to cover edge of pie dish, press it down well and brush with water. Lift rest of dough onto the rolling pin and lay it carefully over the dish. Trim around edge and seal edges of dough with back of a knife. This separates layers so dough puffs up during cooking.

Roll out dough trimmings; cut leaves for decoration. With the point of a knife make a hole in the center of pie (to allow steam to escape) and arrange leaves around it.

Brush dough with beaten egg mixed with a large pinch of salt (adding salt to egg gives pastry a shiny brown glaze). Bake the pastry in heated oven for 25 minutes or until brown. Then wrap a double sheet of foil, or dampened brown paper, over and around the pie; turn down oven to moderate (350°F) and continue baking for ½–1 hour or until meat is tender when pierced with a skewer.

The **traditional English pie dish** is oval and about 2½ inches deep with sloping sides. Any deep baking dish or shallow casserole can be used instead, but it should have an edge at least ½ inch wide to support the pastry cover.

To cover a veal and ham pie: arrange meat in a pie dish, slightly domed, to prevent pastry from falling in during cooking. After rolling out pastry dough to shape of dish, cut an extra strip to cover edge; press this down well (see picture above) and then brush with cold water

Above: lift rest of pastry onto rolling pin and lay over pie

After making a hole in center of pie to allow steam to escape, brush over pastry with beaten egg. Decorate the center with a rose and leaves cut from trimmings; brush with beaten egg

Banbury Cakes

2 cup quantity of flaky pastry, well chilled

For filling
¼ cup butter
1 tablespoon flour
¾ cup currants
2 tablespoons chopped mixed candied peel
½ teaspoon ground allspice, or nutmeg
3 tablespoons sugar
1 tablespoon rum (optional)
1 egg white, beaten
granulated sugar (for sprinkling)

Makes 8–10 cakes.

Method
To make filling: melt butter, blend in flour; cook gently for 2 minutes. Rinse currants and add with candied peel, allspice or nutmeg, sugar and rum, if used; simmer 2–3 minutes. Cool.

Set oven at hot (425°F). Roll out pastry dough to one-eighth inch thickness, turn over and cut large rounds, 5–6 inches in diameter (use a small saucepan lid or saucer as a cutting guide). Put a heaped tablespoon of filling in the center of each round and dampen edges of dough. Draw edges up over filling and seal. Turn cakes over and roll each to an oval, pinching the ends to give the traditional Banbury shape (see page 30).

Make 3 slashes in the top of each cake, place on a baking sheet and bake in heated oven for 15 minutes. Brush cakes with beaten egg white, sprinkle with sugar; continue baking 5 minutes longer or until they are brown and shiny. Sprinkle with sugar again before serving.

Eccles Cakes

2 cup quantity of flaky pastry, well chilled

For filling
2 tablespoons butter
2 tablespoons brown sugar
¾ cup currants
little grated nutmeg, or allspice
2 tablespoons mixed chopped candied peel
1 egg white, beaten
granulated sugar (for sprinkling)

Makes 8–10 cakes.

Method
Set the oven at hot (425°F).

Melt butter and stir in sugar; rinse currants and add, still wet, to mixture with nutmeg, or allspice, and candied peel.

Roll out pastry dough very thinly, turn over and cut into 6 inch circles (use a small saucepan lid or a saucer as a cutting guide). Put a heaped tablespoon of filling in the center of each round and dampen edges of dough. Draw up pastry over filling and pinch together. Turn cakes over and flatten gently with a rolling pin so that the currants just show through, but the cakes are still round. Make 3 small cuts on the top of each cake, brush with egg white and sprinkle with sugar. Place on a baking sheet and bake in heated oven for 15 minutes or until golden.

Tarte Française

2 cup quantity of flaky pastry

For filling
2 oranges
½ cup seedless green grapes
½ cup black grapes, seeded
1 pint strawberries, hulled
2 pears, pared, cored and sliced
2 bananas, sliced
1 egg white, beaten lightly
¾ cup apricot jam glaze

Method
Set oven at hot (400°F); dampen a baking sheet.

Divide pastry into two portions. Roll half to a 12 X 5 inch rectangle about ¼ inch thick. Trim the edges, sprinkle the dough lightly with flour and fold it lengthwise. Cut a rectangle from the center of the dough, leaving a 1 inch border around one long side and both ends. Unfold to form a 'frame'. Roll the remaining dough to a rectangle the same size as the 'frame' and set it on the baking sheet.

Brush a 1 inch border of egg white around the dough (do not allow the egg white to drip down the sides of the dough as this will prevent the pastry from rising). Set the 'frame' on top of the rectangle and press down lightly to seal the dough together. Trim the edges of the dough, if necessary, and flute the edges with the back of a knife (see pastry finishes, Volume 1).

Brush the 'frame' with egg white and prick the center of the dough with a fork to prevent it from rising. Chill 15 minutes, then bake in heated oven for 15–20 minutes or until pastry is puffed and brown. Transfer to a wire rack to cool.

With a serrated-edged knife, cut the peel, pith and outer membrane from the oranges. Cut between the pieces of orange skin to remove the sections, leaving the skin folded back like the pages of a book.

Brush pastry with melted apricot jam glaze, arrange fruit in rows inside the 'frame' and brush the fruit generously with glaze. Let set.

Norfolk Apple Dumplings

2 cup quantity of flaky pastry, well chilled
5 medium-sized tart apples
raspberry jam, or 2 tablespoons butter and 2 tablespoons brown sugar
granulated sugar (for sprinkling)
cream (optional)

Method
Set oven at hot (400°F).

Roll out pastry dough to ¼ inch thickness, turn over and cut into squares large enough for each one to envelop an apple.

Pare and core apples all the way through. Set each one, stalk end down, on a square of dough and fill centers with jam, or the butter and sugar worked together. Dampen the edges of dough, bring corners up to top of apple; pinch together firmly and brush edges lightly with cold water.

Roll out the trimmings of dough and cut into thin strips. Twist these and lay a strip over each join in the dough. Brush apple dumplings with cold water and sprinkle thickly with granulated sugar. Lift onto a baking sheet and bake 20 minutes in heated oven. Lower heat to moderate (350°F); bake 20 minutes longer or until apples are tender when pierced with a skewer. Serve with plain or whipped cream, if you like.

Banbury cake with Eccles cake below (recipes, page 29), and right, rough puff cream horns (recipe, page 32)

Tarte Française is a mouth-watering and colorful flaky pastry (recipe is on page 29)

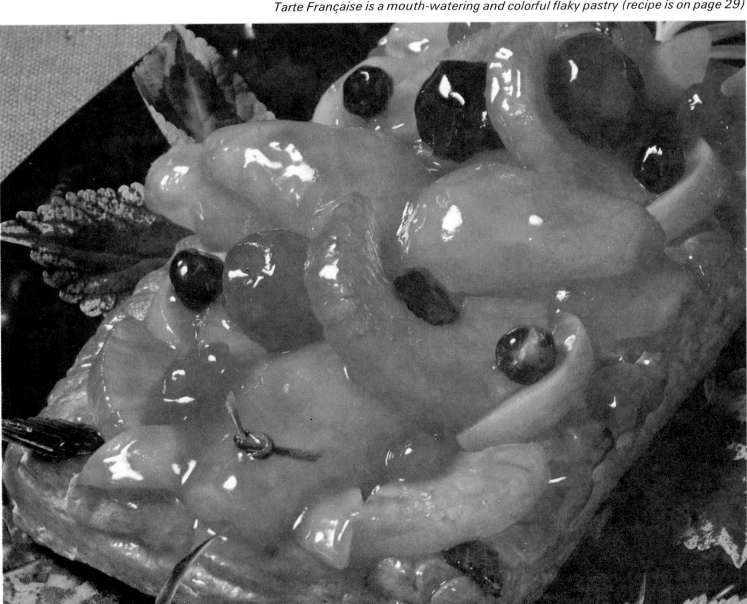

Rough Puff Pastry

Chicken Pie

2 cup quantity of rough puff
    pastry, well chilled
4–5 lb roasting chicken
1 onion, peeled
1 carrot, peeled
bouquet garni
$\frac{1}{2}$ cup white wine
1 quart water
$\frac{1}{2}$ lb large mushrooms
2 tablespoons butter
salt and pepper
small pinch of ground mace
small pinch of cayenne
$\frac{1}{4}$ teaspoon anchovy paste
large bunch of parsley
2 cups velouté sauce
5 tablespoons cream
1 egg, beaten

Deep 9–10 inch pie dish;
    trussing needle and string

Method
Truss the chicken and put with vegetables, bouquet garni, wine and water into a kettle. Cover with a piece of foil (to retain moisture) and the lid and poach over very low heat for $1\frac{1}{2}$ hours or until bird is tender.

Sauté mushrooms whole in butter, season them and add spices and anchovy. Set aside. Cool chicken to tepid in kettle, then drain it, reserving stock for the sauce. Remove meat from bone (discarding the skin) and cut it into medium-sized pieces.

Make a parsley pureé by boiling parsley for 10 minutes in a little water. Drain, press and push it through a strainer or purée it in a blender. Make a velouté sauce and add the cream and parsley purée to it. Sea-son and arrange chicken and mushrooms in layers in the pie dish, moistening well with the sauce.

Leave mixture until cold, then set oven at hot (425°F). Cover with pastry dough as in the veal and ham pie recipe (see page 28). Brush with beaten egg and bake in the heated oven for 30 minutes, or until the pastry is well browned.

Velouté Sauce

For 2 cup quantity: melt 3 tablespoons butter, stir in $2\frac{1}{2}$ tablespoons flour and cook a few seconds until straw colored. Then take from heat, cool slightly and stir in 2 cups chicken stock. Bring to a boil, stirring until thickened and season with salt and pepper. Simmer several minutes until glossy. See also White Sauces on pages 44–45.

Quantity Terms
Terms like '2 cup quantity of pastry' refer to the amount of dough obtained by using 2 cups of flour, *not 2 cups of prepared pastry dough*. As a quantity guide, 2 cup quantity of flaky, or rough puff, pastry will line two 9 inch pie pans, or are enough for a double crust 9 inch pie.

Sausage Rolls

2 cup quantity of rough puff
    pastry
$1\frac{1}{2}$ lb sausagemeat
1 egg, beaten to mix with
    $\frac{1}{2}$ teaspoon salt (for glaze)

Makes about 12 rolls.

Method
Set oven at hot (400°F) and dampen a baking sheet.

Roll out pastry dough to a rectangle about 8 inches wide and $\frac{1}{8}$ inch thick. Trim the edges and cut the dough in half lengthwise.

Divide sausagemeat in half and roll it into 2 cylinders, each as long as the dough; set the sausagemeat on the dough.

Brush the edges of the dough with a little egg glaze and roll it around the sausage-meat, leaving the overlapping edge underneath. Brush rolls again with egg glaze, mark the top in a lattice with the point of a knife, if you like, and cut in 3 inch lengths. Prick the rolls with a fork to allow steam to escape, transfer to the prepared baking sheet and chill 15 minutes.

Bake the rolls in heated oven for 15–20 minutes or until puffed and brown. Transfer to a wire rack to cool.

Cream Horns

2 cup quantity of rough puff
    pastry, well chilled
1 egg white, beaten
strawberry or raspberry jam
$\frac{3}{4}$ cup Chantilly cream
pistachios, finely chopped
    (for decoration)

10–12 cream horn molds;
    pastry bag; large star tube

Method
Lightly grease molds and a baking sheet. Set oven at hot (425°F).

Roll out pastry dough to one-eighth inch thickness, cut into long, 1 inch wide strips and brush with a very little beaten egg white. Wind dough around molds, starting at the point and overlapping each round. Trim tops, brush again with egg white, and set on baking sheet. Bake in heated oven for 8 minutes or until crisp and pale golden.

Remove horns from molds. When cold put a teaspoon of jam in the bottom of each horn and fill with Chantilly cream, preferably using a pastry bag fitted with a large star tube. Decorate top of each with pinch of pistachios.

Chantilly Cream

Whip 1 cup heavy cream until it starts to thicken; add 1 tablespoon sugar and $\frac{1}{2}$ teaspoon vanilla; continue beating until cream holds a shape. (If kitchen is warm and sugar and vanilla are added before first beating, cream will not thicken; so in hot weather, chill cream, bowl and beater before whipping.)

Sausage rolls can be served hot or cold

Fresh haddock mousse is garnished with cucumber twists (recipe is on page 36)

Serve a Stylish Menu

Cold mousse of haddock or delicious scallops start this menu. Baby chickens follow, resplendent in a rich sauce, and a special parfait ends the meal. Follow the Timetable on page 36 and your meal will be a success.

The wines suggested are keyed to the chicken Alsacienne, but are appropriate to the entire meal. As they are relatively inexpensive, it might be fun to purchase both the foreign and domestic editions, and savor them with all three dishes or against one another. The Alsatian Gewürztraminer, raised near France's German border, has a spicy sweetness to the nose, but is rather dry on the palate. The American version is just a shade sweeter, but is every bit as refreshing.

Haddock Mousse
or Scallops

Chicken Alsacienne
Green Beans with Pine Nuts
Boiled Potatoes or Buttered Noodles

Raspberry Parfait

White wine – Gewürztraminer (Alsace)
or Gewürztraminer (California)

TIMETABLE

Day before

Make raspberry purée for parfait; keep in freezing section of refrigerator or in freezer.

Morning

Make haddock mousse, cover mold and refrigerate. Mayonnaise can be made at the same time, covered, and refrigerated. *Or cook scallops and let them stand in their liquid in the refrigerator. Make sauce for scallops given in a covered bowl. Prepare rice and put in a well-buttered baking dish ready for reheating.* Peel new potatoes and stand in cold water. Wash and halve green beans and store in a plastic bag in the refrigerator.
Split chickens and make stock.

Assemble equipment for final cooking from 6:40 p.m. for dinner around 8 p.m.

You will find that **cooking times** given in the individual recipes for these dishes have sometimes been adapted in the timetable to help you when cooking and serving this menu as a party meal.

Order of Work

6:40

Whip cream for parfait, cover, put in refrigerator.
Start cooking chicken.
Cook beans, drain and refresh.

7:15

If preparing parfait in advance, do so now and refrigerate.
Put potatoes to boil.
Cover rice with buttered paper or foil and put in moderate oven to reheat.

7:30

Put chicken in oven to keep warm.
Make sauce for chicken and keep warm in a double boiler.
Unmold mousse onto serving platter, garnish with tomato or cucumber slices and refrigerate.
Drain potatoes, toss in butter and keep warm. *Or start cooking noodles.*

7:45

Toss green beans and pine nuts in butter over heat for 5 minutes; add parsley and seasoning. Keep warm.
Drain and finish noodles just before serving.
If parfait is to be assembled between courses, take raspberry purée from freezing section and put into refrigerator.
Drain scallops and heat in the sauce; arrange in shells with rice just before serving.
Spoon sauce over chicken just before serving.
Whip egg whites; put parfait together just before serving.

Appetizer

Haddock Mousse

1 lb fresh haddock fillet
pinch of salt
6 peppercorns
squeeze of lemon juice

For mousse
1½ cups milk
1 slice of onion
1 bay leaf
6 peppercorns
2 tablespoons butter
1 teaspoon paprika
1½ tablespoons flour
1 envelope gelatin
¼ cup cold water
½ cup heavy cream
1 egg white
salt and pepper

To finish
½ cup mayonnaise
1–2 tablespoons tomato juice
dash of Tabasco
tomato, or cucumber, slices
 (for garnish)

*Plain, or fish-shaped, mold
(1½ quart capacity)*

Method

Set oven at moderate (350°F). Rinse fish in cold water, remove skin; place in a buttered baking dish with salt, peppercorns and lemon juice. Cover dish with buttered paper; bake in heated oven for 12–15 minutes or until the fish flakes easily. Let fish cool. Oil mold lightly.

To make the mousse: heat milk with onion, bay leaf and peppercorns, and let stand until well flavored. Strain. Melt butter in a saucepan. Stir in the paprika and let it cook over low heat for about 1 minute. Remove pan from heat and stir in the flour until smooth. Add strained milk and cook the sauce,

stirring constantly, until it boils. Transfer sauce to a bowl, cover and let cool.

Drain fish and pound it in a bowl with a wooden spoon, potato masher, or pestle; add cold sauce, a little at a time. Then sprinkle gelatin over ¼ cup cold water in a bowl and leave to dissolve for 5 minutes or until the gelatin looks spongy. Stand bowl in a pan of hot water to dissolve gelatin completely. Stir into fish mixture. Whip cream until stiff; in another bowl, beat egg white until it holds a firm peak. Fold both cream and egg white into fish mixture, season well, turn into mold, cover and refrigerate until set.

Just before serving, unmold the mousse onto a serving platter and coat it with mayonnaise mixed with tomato juice and Tabasco sauce, or serve the mayonnaise sauce in a separate dish. Garnish mousse with slices of tomato or cucumber.

Mayonnaise

2 egg yolks
¼ teaspoon salt
pinch of pepper
pinch of dry mustard
¾ cup oil
2 tablespoons wine vinegar

Makes 1 cup.

Method

In a bowl, beat egg yolks and seasonings with a small whisk or wooden spoon until thick. Add oil, drop by drop; when 2 tablespoons have been added, mixture will be very thick. Stir in 1 teaspoon vinegar.

Remaining oil can be added more quickly (1 tablespoon at a time, beaten thoroughly between each addition until smooth, or in a thin steady stream if using an electric blender). When all the oil has been used, add remaining vinegar with more seasoning to taste.

To thin and lighten mayonnaise, add a little hot water. For a coating consistency, thin with a little cream or milk. **Watchpoint:** mayonnaise curdles easily, so be sure to add oil drop by drop at first; and continue adding *very* slowly until very thick, after which you can speed up. If mayonnaise does curdle, start with a fresh yolk in another bowl and work well with seasonings. Then add curdled mixture drop by drop. To lessen chances of curdling, have all ingredients at room temperature before starting.

To twist slices of cucumber: wipe and slice cucumber thinly and make a cut in each slice from the center to the outside edge. Twist one cut edge away from the center to make the slices stand up.

Turn the haddock mousse mixture into a lightly oiled mold before chilling

Alternative Appetizer

Curried Scallops

2 cups (1 pint) sea or bay
   scallops
½ cup water
generous squeeze of lemon
   juice
6 peppercorns
½ bay leaf

For sauce
5 tablespoons boiling water
1 tablespoon ground almonds
2 tablespoons butter
1 small onion, finely chopped
1 teaspoon curry powder
1 tablespoon flour
1 teaspoon tomato paste
½ cup milk
juice of ½ lemon
2 tablespoons heavy cream

To serve
boiled rice (see page 64)
paprika (for garnish)

Bay scallops are a luxury; they have a sweet nut-like flavor that blends superbly with butter and delicate cream sauces. Unfortunately they are scarce and when available they are expensive.
Sea scallops have a similar but more robust flavor and are widely available frozen.

Method
In a saucepan put scallops in water, with lemon juice, peppercorns and bay leaf; bring to a boil. Over low heat, poach sea scallops for 6–7 minutes, or bay scallops for 2 minutes, and let them cool in the liquid.

To make the sauce, pour boiling water over almonds and let stand 10–15 minutes.

Use scallop shells for attractive individual servings

Strain almond 'milk' through several thicknesses of cheesecloth into a bowl, literally squeezing the ground almonds to release all the liquid.

Melt butter in a saucepan, add onion and cook until soft but not colored. Stir in curry powder and flour until smooth and cook over low heat for about 2 minutes. Add tomato paste and milk.

Continue cooking until sauce comes to a boil, then simmer 5 minutes. Add almond 'milk', lemon juice to give a tart flavor and heavy cream. Drain scallops, cut them into quarters (if large sea scallops) and add to sauce.

Serve the scallops in individual deep shells, with boiled rice down one side, and sprinkled with paprika.

Entrée

Chicken Alsacienne

2 chickens (1½–2 lb each)
1 tablespoon oil
2 tablespoons butter
salt and pepper
½ cup white wine
1 cup strong chicken stock
1 teaspoon arrowroot
1 can (2½ oz) pâté de foie
3 tablespoons heavy cream
watercress (for garnish)

Method

Split chickens in half and cut away the backbone and rib cage with kitchen scissors or poultry shears. To make the stock, cook discarded bones with giblets and enough water to cover.

Heat oil in a large skillet, add butter and, when it starts to foam, put in chickens, skin side down. Season with salt and pepper to taste, and cook over low heat for 15–20 minutes or until golden brown. Turn the birds, sprinkle with half the wine, cover and continue cooking very gently for 20–30 minutes or until tender. Transfer chickens to a platter and keep warm.

Stir remaining wine into the skillet and bring to a boil, scraping bottom and sides of pan to remove the browned juices. Boil to reduce the liquid by half. Stir arrowroot into half the chicken stock to make a smooth paste and reserve. Work pâté de foie through a strainer and mix it with remaining stock. Add arrowroot paste to pan juices and cook over a low heat, stirring constantly, until the sauce thickens. Strain it into a small saucepan, add pâté mixture and heavy cream. Reheat gently, adjust seasoning, if necessary, and spoon sauce over chicken. Garnish with watercress.

Serve with boiled new potatoes or buttered noodles, and green beans with pine nuts.

Above: remove backbone from the split chickens with scissors or poultry shears.

Below: cut away the rib cage before making the stock with the bones and giblets

Accompaniments to Entrée

Buttered Noodles

½ lb noodles
2 tablespoons butter
salt
black pepper, freshly ground

Method

Cook noodles in plenty of boiling salted water, 2–3 quarts at least, for 8–10 minutes. Stir gently from time to time to prevent the noodles from sticking to the bottom of the pan. When cooked, they should look creamy and opaque and can be severed with a thumbnail (or taste one to see if done).

Watchpoint: do not overcook the noodles as they become sticky and pasty.

Pour at once into a colander, rinse in hot water and drain well. Rinse the pan used to cook the noodles and add the butter. Return noodles to the pan and toss over low heat for 1–2 minutes. Season with salt and black pepper.

If the noodles must be kept hot before serving, pour about 1 cup hot water into the pan, put in the drained noodles, cover and keep warm at the side of the stove. When ready to serve, drain off the water, add butter and seasonings and toss.

Green Beans with Pine Nuts

1 lb green beans
½ cup pine nuts
2 tablespoons butter
1 tablespoon chopped parsley
salt and pepper

Method

Trim the beans and leave them whole, if they are small, or halve them if they are large. Cook them in boiling salted water for 10–15 minutes or until just tender, drain, refresh and drain again.

Melt the butter, add the beans and pine nuts; cook over medium heat, tossing the beans carefully, until very hot and well coated with butter. Add the parsley and seasoning and pile in a hot serving dish.

Chicken Alsacienne is named for the pâté de foie which is used in the sauce. Liver pâté, particularly when made of goose liver, is a specialty of Alsace in northeastern France.

Chicken Alsacienne, with sauce spooned over the top, is garnished with watercress

Raspberry parfait at the point of perfection; see watchpoint on opposite page for correct timing

Dessert

Raspberry Parfait

**1 pint fresh, or 1 package
frozen, red raspberries,
preferably without sugar
2 egg whites
½ cup sugar
1½ cups heavy cream**

Method

Work raspberries through a fine strainer, or purée them in a blender and strain to remove the seeds. Put the purée in an ice cube tray or shallow container, cover with foil and freeze overnight.

About an hour before serving, beat egg whites until they hold a soft shape. Gradually beat in the sugar until the mixture holds a stiff peak. Whip the cream in a separate bowl until you can see the path of the beater.

Remove frozen raspberry purée from the freezer and work it with a wooden spoon to break down the ice crystals, or transfer to a bowl and beat with a whisk.

Fold whipped cream and egg whites together, then quickly but carefully fold in the semi-frozen raspberry purée. Pile the parfait into tall glasses or a crystal bowl and keep in the coldest part of the refrigerator until needed.

Watchpoint: the parfait is at its best if put together just before serving. With everything ready — the chilled bowl or glasses, the cream already whipped and waiting in the refrigerator — you can beat the egg whites and sugar and put the whole dessert together in about 8 minutes. Then you'll have the satisfaction of knowing that the parfait is being served when it is at the point of perfection.

Above: for raspberry parfait, beat the egg whites and sugar mixture to just the right consistency

Below: gently fold the raspberry purée into the beaten egg whites and whipped cream

Layered Parfaits

Parfaits can be served plain, as in this recipe, or they are often layered in tall glasses with ingredients of contrasting colors.

Crushed meringues are a favorite and ladyfingers soaked in kirsch or orange-flavored liqueur are excellent in a fruit parfait.

One or two layers of chocolate sauce make a dramatic contrast in a vanilla or coffee parfait, and sweetened chestnut purée is good in a vanilla or chocolate parfait.

Layered parfaits should be crowned with a large rosette of whipped cream and kept in the freezer until serving. Most mixtures can be prepared several weeks ahead.

How to make Sauces

Sauces are the foundation of French cooking but there is no mystery to their making – this simply depends on a perfect balance of ingredients. If proportion of flour to liquid is wrong, no amount of cooking will give a sauce the right consistency.

An inventive sauce can transform a simple dish into something superlative and, once you are familiar with the 'mother' (mère) sauces you can make an infinite number of variations. Sauces fall into three groups – white sauces with white, velouté and béchamel as 'mother' sauces; brown sauces with Espagnole as the 'mother' sauce, and butter sauces with Hollandaise, Béarnaise and sauce blanche au beurre as 'mother' sauces. Some of these sauces appear elsewhere but, to make this lesson complete, we are repeating them or versions of them.

We also discuss liaisons in greater detail; these are mainly used for making white and brown sauces from liquids and gravies.

Points to remember

1 The volume of fat and flour should be equal to give a soft, semi-liquid roux (the foundation of a flour sauce).

2 If the roux is hot, the liquid should be warm or cold; if the roux is cold, the liquid must be warm. This makes blending easier and avoids a granular texture.

3 For a **béchamel**, or **white**, sauce, melt fat gently (do not let it sizzle), take from heat and stir in the flour (to make a white roux).

For a **velouté** sauce, cook flour in the fat over a low heat for a few seconds until it is a pale straw color (a blond roux) before adding liquid.

For a **brown** sauce, cook the flour in the fat over low to medium heat for several minutes, stirring occasionally with a wire whisk, until the flour is a rich brown (a brown roux).

4 The fats used may be butter, margarine, meat drippings or oil, according to the type of sauce being made.

Consistencies
The proportion of flour to liquid in a sauce can vary its thickness for the following different uses.

Flowing: for serving as an accompanying sauce – 1 tablespoon butter and 1 tablespoon flour to 1 cup liquid.

Coating: slightly thicker consistency for coating fillets of fish, eggs and vegetables – $1\frac{1}{2}$ tablespoons butter and $1\frac{1}{2}$ tablespoons flour to 1 cup liquid.

Panada: thick sauce for binding, which is used as a base for croquettes, fish or meat mousses – 3–4 tablespoons butter and 3–4 tablespoons flour to 1 cup liquid.

Liaisons
Liaisons play an important part in the making of sauces. The word itself means a binding together and refers to ingredients which are used to thicken sauces and soups.

There are various ways to bind sauces:
1 Kneaded butter (beurre manié) is a liaison mixture of butter and flour in the proportions of almost twice as much butter as flour, worked together on a plate with a fork to make a paste. It is added in small pieces to thicken the liquid in which food has been cooked, i.e. fish stews, casseroles, etc.

This is a useful liaison to use when quantity of liquid remaining in a dish is unknown, thereby making it difficult to estimate how much flour alone should be used for thickening.

Kneaded butter should be added to hot (but not boiling)

White Sauces

liquids. Shake pan gently and when butter has melted (indicating flour has been absorbed into the liquid), reboil. If the liquid still is not thick enough, repeat the process.

2 Fécule, i.e. arrowroot or potato starch, should be mixed to a smooth paste with water or milk and stirred into the nearly boiling liquid off the heat. Once added, bring just to a boil and remove from heat. Use with ragoûts and casseroles as well as brown sauces.

3 Cornstarch can be used instead of arrowroot or potato starch but gives a slightly heavier result (most often used for sweet dishes, e.g. custard). It is added in the same way but must be simmered 3 minutes to cook thoroughly.

4 A mixture of egg yolks and cream may be used to thicken and enrich velouté sauces and some cream soups. The yolk or yolks are worked thoroughly together with the cream and 2–3 tablespoons of sauce are stirred in, a little at a time. When well blended, this mixture is gradually stirred into the main bulk of the sauce which is then stirred continuously over low heat. This allows the egg yolks to cook slowly and gives a particularly creamy consistency to the sauce. Never boil the sauce or it will curdle.

White Sauce

1½ tablespoons butter
1½ tablespoons flour
1 cup milk
salt and pepper

A white sauce, made in exactly the same proportions as béchamel but without flavoring the milk, is quick and easy. It can be a base for cheese, onion or other sauces with a pronounced flavor. Béchamel is better for more delicate sauces like mushroom and egg. Makes 1 cup.

Method
Melt butter in a small pan, take from heat and stir in flour. Blend in half the milk, then add the rest. Stir this over moderate heat until boiling and then let it simmer for 1–2 minutes. Season to taste with salt and pepper.

Béchamel Sauce

1 cup milk
1 slice of onion
1 small bay leaf
6 peppercorns
1 blade of mace, or pinch of ground mace

For roux
1½ tablespoons butter
1½ tablespoons flour
salt and pepper

This basic recipe for béchamel sauce (white roux base with flavored milk added) can be used to make mornay (cheese), soubise (onion), mushroom or egg sauces. Proportions of ingredients may vary according to consistency required. Makes 1 cup.

Method
In a covered saucepan infuse milk with flavorings by heating it almost to boiling and keeping hot for 5–7 minutes. Strain milk and reserve. Clean pan and melt butter in it. Remove from heat and stir in flour to make a white roux (which should be soft and semi-liquid).

Pour on half the milk through a strainer; blend until smooth with a whisk or wooden spoon. Add remaining milk, season lightly; bring to a boil over low to moderate heat, stirring continuously. Simmer 2 minutes only to cook flour.

Watchpoint: if sauce begins to look lumpy when bringing to a boil, smooth it out by vigorously stirring or beating with a wire whisk, provided sauce has not been boiled. To do this, draw pan aside, stir hard, then return to heat. Simmer 1–2 minutes. If sauce has boiled, the only remedy is to strain it.

Mushroom Sauce

½ cup (2 oz) mushrooms

For béchamel sauce
1 cup flavored milk (see basic recipe, left)
2 tablespoons butter
1½ tablespoons flour
salt and pepper

Serve with eggs, fish and chicken.

Method
Wash mushrooms, drain and chop them. Prepare flavored milk. Cook mushrooms in half the butter for 2–3 minutes until tender and fairly dry. Take from heat, add remaining butter and, when melted, stir in the flour. Season and blend in the milk. Stir over medium heat until boiling and cook 2 minutes.

Egg Sauce

2 eggs, hard-cooked and
   finely chopped

For béchamel sauce
1½ tablespoons butter
1½ tablespoons flour
1 cup flavored milk (see
   basic recipe on page 45)
salt and pepper

Serve with poached fish.
Makes 1½ cups.

Method
Make béchamel sauce, stir in
eggs and season well.

Mornay (Cheese) Sauce

¼ cup grated cheese
½ teaspoon prepared mustard
   (regular, or Dijon-style)
1 cup well-seasoned white,
   or béchamel, sauce

The cheese can be a mix-
ture of Gruyère and Parmesan
or a dry Cheddar. If using
Gruyère, which thickens
sauce, reduce basic roux to 1
tablespoon each of butter and
flour. If still too thick, add a
little milk. Serve with eggs,
fish, chicken and vegetables.
Makes 1 cup.

Method
Make white or béchamel
sauce, remove from heat and
gradually stir in grated cheese.
When well mixed, add mus-
tard. Reheat but do not boil.

Soubise (Onion) Sauce

2 large onions, sliced
2 tablespoons butter
1 tablespoon cream (optional)
salt and pepper
1 cup white, or béchamel,
   sauce (use 2 tablespoons
   each of butter and flour
   for the roux)

Serve with eggs and veal.
Makes 1½ cups.

Method
Blanch onion slices by putting
in cold water, bringing to a
boil and draining. Then melt
the butter in a pan, add onion
and cook, covered, until
tender but not colored. To
help prevent coloring, press
a piece of buttered paper
or foil on the onion slices.
Remove from the pan and
push through a nylon strainer,
or purée them in a blender.
   Add the puréed onion to a
hot white or béchamel sauce,
stir in the cream, if used, and
season well.

Velouté Sauce

1½ tablespoons butter
1½ tablespoons flour
1–1¼ cups stock
¼ cup light cream
salt and pepper
squeeze of lemon juice

For liaison (optional)
1 egg yolk, lightly beaten
2 tablespoons heavy cream

This sauce is made with a
blond roux. The liquid added
can be strong stock (made
from veal, chicken or fish
bones, according to dish with
which sauce is being served),
or liquid in which food was
simmered or poached.
   Velouté sauces are a base
for others, such as caper,
mustard, parsley, poulette or
suprême (the last two are
advanced sauces; recipes will
be given in a future Volume).
Makes ¾–1 cup.

Method
Melt butter in a saucepan,
stir in flour and cook for about
5 seconds until roux is the
color of pale straw (blond
roux). Remove from heat and
cool slightly before stirring
in the stock.
   Blend, return to heat and
stir until thick. Add light
cream, season and bring to a
boil. Cook 4–5 minutes, or
until sauce is glossy and the
consistency of heavy cream.
If using a liaison, mix egg
yolk and cream and stir in a
little warm sauce; stir carefully back into remaining
sauce and reheat until it thickens slightly. Add lemon juice
and take pan from heat.
Watchpoint: do not allow the
sauce to boil after the liaison
has been added or it will
curdle.

Caper Sauce

1½ tablespoons drained capers
2 teaspoons chopped parsley
1 cup velouté sauce

Serve with lamb or poached
fish. Makes 1 cup.

Method
Make 1 cup velouté sauce.
Stir in capers and parsley.

Mustard Sauce

1 teaspoon prepared mustard
   (regular, or Dijon-style)
1 cup velouté sauce

Serve with poached fish,
broiled mackerel and herring.
Makes 1 cup.

Method
Make velouté sauce. Mix
mustard with 1 tablespoon
sauce; stir into remaining
sauce.

Parsley Sauce

bunch of fresh parsley,
   stalks removed
1 cup velouté sauce

Serve with eggs, fish or
boiled chicken. Makes 1 cup.

Method
Make velouté sauce. Wash
parsley sprigs, boil for 7
minutes in salted water;
drain and dry with paper
towels. Push through a wire
strainer (or purée in a blender
with a little of the sauce)
and beat into the hot velouté
sauce.

Brown Sauces

You can improvise a brown sauce to serve with chops or hamburgers simply from homemade stock or a can of bouillon. But the brown sauce which is called a 'sauce mère' (a mother sauce from which other sauces are derived – as with a béchamel or velouté sauce) is a French classic.

When the famous French chef Carême (who was in his time chief cook to Napoleon, Tsar Nicholas of Russia and George IV of England) made his demi-Espagnole sauce, he described it as 'gradually taking on that brilliant glaze which delights the eye when it first appears...'

The recipe has scarcely changed and today the same brilliant glaze denotes the perfect sauce. From this 'mother' sauce, a large number of advanced sauces can be made.

Points to remember

1 To create the perfect sauce, every detail must be right and this will take time and trouble. However, brown sauces keep well for up to a week in the refrigerator, so make double or triple quantity and store the excess in a covered container.

2 Much depends on the stock with which the sauce is made. For a good flavor and a fine, glossy texture, use clear brown bone stock that is free of grease and set to a light but not too firm jellied consistency.

3 Whisk the sauce briskly when it first comes to a boil and is thickening, until it is very smooth. Once simmering starts, stir gently only when necessary, as whisking will cloud the finished sauce.

4 Do not add more flour than stated in the recipe. The consistency of the finished sauce should be that of heavy cream and the 'half-glaze' is achieved by reduction of the bone stock in the sauce, rather than by the addition of extra flour. (Flour is used at the beginning only to absorb the fat and bind the ingredients together.)

Basic Brown (Espagnole) Sauce

6 tablespoons oil
1 onion, finely diced
1 carrot, finely diced
1 stick of celery, finely diced
3 tablespoons flour
1 teaspoon tomato paste
2 tablespoons chopped mushroom stalks, or
   1 mushroom, chopped
5 cups well-flavored brown stock
bouquet garni
salt and pepper

When serving broiled steak, a tablespoon of Espagnole sauce, added to a gravy or mixed with the juices in the broiler pan, makes a delicious accompaniment. Makes 2 cups.

Method

In a saucepan, heat oil and add diced vegetables (there should be no more than 6 tablespoons of vegetables in all). Lower the heat and cook gently until the vegetables are transparent and about to start browning. They will shrink slightly at this point.

Stir in the flour and brown it slowly, stirring occasionally with a wire whisk or metal spoon and scraping the flour well from the bottom of the pan. When it is brown, take from heat and cool slightly.

Watchpoint: the flour should be cooked until dark brown, but do not allow it to burn.

Stir in the tomato paste, chopped mushroom, 4 cups cold stock, bouquet garni and seasoning.

Bring to a boil, whisking constantly, partly cover the pan and cook gently for 35–40 minutes. During this time skim off any scum that rises to the surface. Then add half the remaining stock, bring again to a boil and skim. Simmer 5 minutes, add the remaining stock, bring to a boil and skim again. (The addition of cold stock accelerates the rising of scum and so helps to clear the sauce.)

Cook 5 minutes longer, then strain, pressing vegetables gently to extract the juice. Clean pan and return sauce to it. Partly cover pan and continue to simmer sauce until it is very glossy and the consistency of heavy cream. It is now ready to be used alone or as a base for any of the following sauces.

Sauce Demi-glace

¼ cup (1 oz) chopped mushrooms
2 teaspoons tomato paste
2 cups Espagnole sauce
¼ cup jellied stock
¼ cup sherry
1 tablespoon butter

Serve with dark meats. Makes 2 cups.

Method

Stir mushrooms into tomato paste and add both to prepared Espagnole sauce in a pan. Simmer 5 minutes, add stock and continue to simmer uncovered, skimming often, until well reduced. Add sherry and beat in the butter. Do not boil after this, but reheat or keep warm in a water bath (see page 92).

Sauce Bigarade

1 bitter (Seville) orange
1 tablespoon butter
1 shallot or scallion finely chopped
¾ cup red Burgundy wine
1 small bay leaf
1 cup Espagnole sauce
2 teaspoons red currant jelly
squeeze of lemon juice

Serves with duck, venison or pork. Makes 1 cup.

Method

In a small pan melt butter, add shallot, cover and cook gently for 1 minute. Add wine, bay leaf and peeled rind of ½ the orange. Simmer to reduce by about a quarter. Strain into the prepared Espagnole sauce, add the red currant jelly and dissolve it over low heat.

Peel remaining orange rind with a sharp knife and cut into thin strips, then blanch in boiling water for 5 minutes, drain and add to the sauce. Cut the skin and white pith from the orange and cut out the sections. Squeeze the inner skin to remove any juice and add to sauce with lemon juice. Simmer 4–5 minutes and then add the orange sections. Reheat without boiling.

Bigarade is the French name for the bitter Seville orange which is used to make marmalade. For sauce bigarade, you can replace the bitter orange with a sweet one, adding extra lemon juice for sharpness, but instead of the sweet segments use the juice of half the orange.

Sauce Bordelaise

1 cup red Bordeaux wine
2 shallots, or scallions, finely chopped
small sprig of thyme, or 1 pinch of dried thyme
small bay leaf
1 cup Espagnole sauce (preferably made with white bone stock)
little extra bone stock
1 teaspoon arrowroot (mixed to a paste with 1 tablespoon stock)
1–2 marrow bones, or 1½ tablespoons butter

Serve with broiled or roast beef. Makes 1 cup.

Method

Put shallots, wine and herbs into a pan, simmer to reduce by about one-third, then add to the prepared Espagnole sauce. Bring to a boil and simmer 6–7 minutes, skimming well. Add a little cold stock to help skimming. When the flavor is strong and good, thicken, if necessary, with the arrowroot paste. Strain into a clean pan and keep warm.

With a knife dipped in hot water, scoop marrow from the bone and cut into small cubes. Poach 6–7 minutes in simmering water. Drain carefully on paper towels and add to the sauce just before serving.

If marrow is not available, stir the butter in small pieces briskly into the sauce just before serving.

> **Bordelaise** is applied to many different dishes and means that red or white wine is used, together with beef marrow.

Sauce Chasseur

½ cup (2 oz) sliced small mushrooms
1 shallot, or scallion, finely chopped
1 tablespoon butter
½ cup white wine
1 teaspoon tomato paste
1 cup Espagnole sauce

Serve with all meats and with broiled or roasted chicken. Makes 1 cup.

Method

Cook shallot in butter in a pan for 1 minute, add mushrooms and cook 2 minutes before adding the wine. Simmer to reduce by one-third, then add to the prepared Espagnole sauce with the tomato paste. Simmer 3–4 minutes before using.

Sauce Madère

¼ cup Madeira
2 teaspoons tomato paste
2 cups Espagnole sauce
¼ cup jellied stock
1 tablespoon butter

Serve with roast/braised fillet of beef, lamb cutlets, veal escalopes, or chicken. Makes 2 cups.

Method

Stir tomato paste into prepared Espagnole sauce, simmer 5 minutes and add the stock. Continue to simmer, uncovered, skimming often, until well reduced. Add wine and beat in the butter. Do not boil after this, but keep warm or reheat when necessary in a water bath (see page 92).

Sauce Périgueux

2 cups sauce Madère
small can whole truffles or truffle pieces
2 tablespoons butter
salt and pepper
squeeze of lemon juice (optional)

Serve with roast beef or broiled steak.

Method

Drain the truffles, reserving the liquid, and if using whole ones, cut them in thin slices or julienne strips. Add truffles and the liquid to the sauce Madère and simmer 5 minutes.

Take sauce from the heat and whisk in the butter, a few pieces at a time. Taste the sauce for seasoning and add a little lemon juice if you like.

Watchpoint: do not reheat the sauce or it may curdle.

Sauce Robert

2 cups Espagnole sauce
½ onion, finely chopped
¼ cup white wine vinegar
½ cup white wine
2 tablespoons gherkin pickles, cut in strips
½ teaspoon Dijon-style mustard
1 tablespoon butter

Serve with pork.

Method

Sauté the onion in half the butter until soft but not browned. Add the wine vinegar and wine and boil until it is reduced to ¼ cup. Add the Espagnole sauce and simmer 15 minutes or until well flavored. Add gherkin pickles, bring sauce just back to a boil and take from the heat. Stir in the mustard and remaining butter.

Watchpoint: do not allow the sauce to boil again or it may curdle.

Butter
Sauces

Hollandaise sauce is ideal for serving with poached fish

Butter sauces are always served lukewarm.

The best known butter sauces are Hollandaise and Béarnaise. Besides being served alone, a small quantity of Hollandaise is often added to a velouté or béchamel sauce for coating fish or delicate meats such as veal or chicken. Hollandaise sauce has an egg yolk base to which butter is added with lemon juice as seasoning (or vinegar, reduced so as to mellow the flavor). Béarnaise sauce is similar to Hollandaise but is sharper and flavored with herbs.

Sauce blanche au beurre (white sauce with butter) is less widely known. Made with a butter and flour roux to which boiling water and butter are added, with lemon juice as seasoning, it is served with white meats, veal or chicken, or it can form the base of a Venetian sauce (sauce Vénitienne) — sometimes called green sauce (sauce verte). Sauce blanche au beurre can become 'mock Hollandaise' (sauce bâtarde) with the addition of 1—2 egg yolks, and is more economical and handles easier than true Hollandaise.

Points to remember

1 The usual proportion of egg to butter in Hollandaise sauce is 1 egg yolk to $\frac{1}{4}$ cup butter; more butter may be added, but beyond a certain point the yolk will not absorb this and sauce will separate. If too little butter is added, sauce will taste eggy.

2 All butter sauces curdle easily and they must be cooked over gentle heat or, for Hollandaise and Béarnaise, in a water bath or double boiler with the water hot but not boiling. Butter sauces with a flour base are much less likely to curdle than those with an egg yolk base, but they still must be treated with care.

3 If Hollandaise or Béarnaise sauce is too thin, gentle heating will thicken it. If very thick, this is a danger signal, so take sauce from heat at once. If sauce does curdle, do not stir but take off the heat and drop in an ice cube. Leave to cool a little, then stir gently. If sauce is still curdled, start from the beginning again, adding curdled mixture instead of butter to more fresh egg yolks.

4 All these sauces can be stored in airtight containers in the refrigerator for several days. If storing Hollandaise or adding it to another sauce, omit cream given in the recipe.

5 All these sauces should be reheated or kept hot in a water bath or double boiler using hot, not boiling water.

Hollandaise Sauce

$\frac{1}{4}$ **cup white wine vinegar (seasoned with 6 peppercorns, 1 blade of mace, 1 slice of onion, and 1 small bay leaf)**
3 egg yolks
$\frac{3}{4}$ **cup unsalted butter**
salt and pepper
1—2 tablespoons light cream, or milk
squeeze of lemon juice (optional)

Makes 1 cup.

Method

In a small pan boil vinegar with its seasonings until reduced to a scant tablespoon. Set aside.

With a wooden spoon, beat egg yolks in a bowl with $\frac{1}{2}$ tablespoon butter and a pinch of salt until light and slightly thick. Strain on the vinegar, set bowl on a pan of boiling water, turn off heat and add remaining butter in small pieces, stirring vigorously all the time.

Watchpoint: when adding the butter, it should be slightly soft, not chilled.

When all the butter has been added and sauce is thick, add cream or milk and lemon juice and taste for seasoning. Sauce should be pleasantly sharp yet bland and should have the consistency of heavy cream.

Note: Hollandaise sauce is often flavored with lemon juice, but the version above uses seasoned, reduced vinegar to add a mellow touch to the sauce. If you prefer to flavor with lemon juice, omit the vinegar and spices and add lemon juice to taste to the finished sauce.

Blender Hollandaise Sauce

Hollandaise, Béarnaise and all their derivatives can be made quickly and easily in a blender.

Use the same ingredients as for regular Hollandaise sauce and reduce the vinegar in the same way. In a blender put egg yolks with a pinch of salt and blend 30 seconds on medium speed. Heat butter until it is very hot and stops spluttering (do not allow it to brown). With blender at medium speed, add about one-third of the butter in a very slow stream. When mixture is quite thick, strain in vinegar and continue adding butter slowly, increasing blender speed, if necessary, as mixture thickens. When butter is added and sauce is thick, blend in cream and lemon juice and taste for seasoning. If you like, lemon juice may be used in place of the reduced vinegar.

Meat glaze is made from strained brown bone stock, boiled for a fairly long time until it is thick, glossy and brown. The finished glaze will set to a firm jellied consistency and can be stored for several months in a covered container in the refrigerator.

Sauce Maltaise

Make 1 cup Hollandaise sauce, omitting the vinegar and flavorings. Add 2–3 tablespoons orange juice instead of lemon juice and taste sauce for seasoning.

If possible, blood oranges, with red flesh and juice, should be used to give the sauce a deep pink color.

To complete the sauce, add 1 tablespoon of needle-like shreds of orange rind, blanched in boiling water for 5 minutes and then drained. Serve with eggs and fish.

Mousseline Sauce

2 egg yolks
6 tablespoons unsalted butter, slightly softened
juice of $\frac{1}{2}$ lemon
salt and pepper
$\frac{1}{4}$ cup heavy cream

Serve this sauce separately with asparagus, lamb chops and salmon. Makes 1 cup.

Method
Put yolks into a bowl, add $\frac{1}{2}$ tablespoon butter and stand the bowl in a water bath. Beat until the mixture is thick, add lemon juice and season lightly. Beat in remaining butter, piece by piece. When sauce is thick, take from heat and beat 1–2 minutes. Whip cream until it holds a soft shape, fold in, and season.

Béarnaise Sauce

3 tablespoons wine vinegar
6 peppercorns
$\frac{1}{2}$ bay leaf
1 blade of mace
1 slice of onion
2 egg yolks
$\frac{1}{2}$ cup butter
salt and pepper
1 teaspoon meat glaze
1 teaspoon tarragon
1 teaspoon chervil
1 teaspoon chopped parsley
pinch of chopped chives, or little grated onion

This quantity is enough for topping steaks or chops for 4 people, but should be increased by half as much again for a sauce to be served separately. Makes $\frac{3}{4}$ cup.

Method
Put vinegar, peppercorns, bay leaf, mace and slice of onion into a pan; boil until reduced to 1 tablespoon. Set aside.

Place yolks in a small bowl with $\frac{1}{2}$ tablespoon butter and a pinch of salt and beat until thick. Strain in vinegar, set bowl on a pan of boiling water, turn off heat and stir until beginning to thicken.

Add remaining softened butter in small pieces, beating well after each addition. Add meat glaze, herbs and chives or grated onion and season with pepper. Finished sauce should have the consistency of whipped cream.

Sauce Choron

Make $\frac{3}{4}$ cup Béarnaise sauce but omit the tarragon and chervil when adding the meat glaze, parsley and chives. Instead beat in 2 tablespoons tomato paste.

Served with broiled steak or poached salmon.

Sauce Beurre Blanc

3 shallots, chopped
3 tablespoons dry white wine
3 tablespoons white wine vinegar
$\frac{3}{4}$ cup unsalted butter, softened
salt and pepper

This sauce is even simpler than Hollandaise as it contains no eggs. The butter should melt without being oily, so the sauce is smooth and slightly thick. It is a specialty of the Loire valley in France, and is made with the local Sancerre wine. Locally the sauce is served with pike, but it is good with any poached fish.

Method
The shallots must be so finely chopped that they are almost a purée. Put the shallots with the wine and vinegar in a heavy-based pan and simmer until reduced to about 1 teaspoon. Add 1 tablespoon butter and whisk until it is soft but not oily. Continue adding tablespoons of butter until all is added. Keep a bowl of cold water handy to cool the pan quickly if it gets too hot. The sauce should be warm not hot. Taste for seasoning and serve at once.

If necessary, keep the sauce warm over very low heat or in a water bath, but do not heat it too much or it will turn oily.

Genevoise Sauce

5 tablespoons butter
1 tablespoon flour
1 cup court bouillon (from fish with which sauce is to be served), or light stock
2 egg yolks
1–2 tablespoons light cream
2–3 anchovy fillets, soaked in milk (optional)
2 teaspoons anchovy paste
2 teaspoons chopped parsley
pepper

Serve separately with poached or broiled fish. Makes 1½ cups.

Method

Melt 1½ tablespoons of the butter in a pan, stir in flour and pour on court bouillon or stock. Bring to a boil, stirring, and simmer 2–3 minutes.

Mix egg yolks and cream in a bowl; drain and crush the anchovy fillets with paste (if omitting the fillets, use a little more anchovy paste).

Take sauce from heat and combine a little with the yolk mixture. Stir this back into bulk of sauce. Beat in remaining butter in small pieces with the anchovy; add parsley and pepper to taste. Reheat carefully without boiling.

Sauce Blanche au Beurre

¼ cup butter
1 tablespoon flour
1 cup boiling water
good squeeze of lemon juice
salt and pepper

Makes 1¼ cups.

Method

In a saucepan melt 1 tablespoon butter, stir in flour off the heat and, when smooth, pour on all the boiling water,

stirring or whisking briskly all the time.

Stir in the remaining butter in small pieces, whisking between each addition. Add lemon juice and season.

Watchpoint: if water is really boiling it cooks the flour sufficiently. Never bring this sauce to a boil as it gives an unpleasant gluey taste.

Sauce Bâtarde (Mock Hollandaise Sauce)

To the sauce blanche au beurre, beat in 1–2 egg yolks after boiling water has been added. Add remaining butter in small pieces, with lemon juice and seasoning.

Caper Sauce

To the finished sauce blanche au beurre add 2 tablespoons coarsley chopped capers and 2 teaspoons chopped parsley. If you like, add 1 egg yolk as for sauce bâtarde.

Note: alternative recipes for caper and mustard sauces with a velouté sauce base were given on page 46.

Mustard Sauce

To the finished sauce blanche au beurre add 2 teaspoons Dijon-style mustard, or 1 teaspoon regular prepared mustard, per cup of sauce. If you like, add 1 egg yolk as for sauce bâtarde.

Ravigote Sauce

1 cup sauce bâtarde (mock Hollandaise)
1 shallot, finely chopped
2 tablespoons wine vinegar
1 tablespoon butter
½ teaspoon Dijon-style mustard
2 teaspoons chopped mixed herbs (tarragon, chives and parsley)

Serve with sautéed pork chops, salmon and fried fish. Makes 1 cup.

Method

Prepare mock Hollandaise sauce and set aside.

In a pan simmer shallot with vinegar and butter for 2–3 minutes or until soft. Add to sauce with mustard and herbs and reheat gently. This sauce should be slightly sharp and well flavored with the herbs.

Sauce Vénitienne (Venetian Sauce)

1 small cucumber, peeled, seeded and diced
¼ package of frozen spinach, thawed, or 2–3 oz fresh spinach, washed
sprig of tarragon or ½ teaspoon dried tarragon
sprig of chervil or ½ teaspoon dried chervil
5 tablespoons butter
2 teaspoons flour
1 cup water
salt and pepper
2 egg yolks
2 shallots or scallions, finely chopped
½ cup court bouillon (from fish with which sauce is to be served) or light stock

Serve with poached or broiled fish.

Method

Blanch the cucumber in boiling salted water for 3 minutes, drain and reserve. Cook the fresh spinach with the herbs in boiling salted water for 5 minutes; cook the frozen spinach according to the package directions. Drain, squeeze spinach and herbs in a piece of cheesecloth, or the end of a clean dish towel, to remove all moisture, then work through a strainer or purée in a blender.

In a pan melt 1 tablespoon of the butter and stir in the flour. Whisk in water with a little salt and pepper, bring just to a boil and take from heat. Beat in egg yolks and remaining butter, a small piece at a time. Add spinach and herb purée and keep warm in a water bath or the top of a double boiler.

In a saucepan boil shallots or scallions with court bouillon or stock until reduced to ¼ cup. Stir into sauce and taste for seasoning.

HOW TO FRY

Frying is simple and quick to do, but its very speed makes it somewhat tricky. If fried at too high a temperature, food is dry and tasteless; if fried too slowly it becomes sodden with fat. Properly fried food is light, crisp and full of flavor which has been sealed in by hot fat.

Frying can be done in shallow or deep fat. Both methods cover a wide range of basic foods — meat, fish and made-up dishes like croquettes.

On the following pages the correct coatings are described with step-by-step photographs of how to handle egg and breadcrumbs, and how to make fritter batters.

All fried foods are best eaten at once and deep-fried dishes, particularly, lose their crispness on standing and so become unappetizing.

Sizzling hot French fried potatoes are crisp and golden (recipe is on page 60)

Temperature Guide to Frying

Uncooked doughs — fried on a rising temperature, e.g. piroshki, choux pastry (see future Volume)	325°F–375°F
Fish fillets and cooked mixtures, e.g. croquettes	350°F–375°F
Meat	350°F–375°F
French fries, potato chips — first frying second frying	350°F 360°F–375°F
Fritters, sweet and savory	350°F–375°F

Shallow Fat Frying

This is the most common frying method and, as the name implies, is done in a frying pan or skillet, in butter, oil, a mixture of butter and oil, meat drippings, lard or shortening. Foods like small whole fish or fish fillets, lamb chops and made-up mixtures are suited to shallow fat frying.

For the best taste and browning effect use butter; if using an oil and butter mixture the butter adds flavor and oil helps stop butter from burning. When frying with meat drippings, do not coat food in egg and crumbs as the drippings will over-brown the egg.

The amount of fat in the pan is important; it should come halfway up the food to be fried so the sides are completely browned.

Turn the food once only and cook on a moderate to brisk heat (depending on what is being fried and whether it is raw or cooked when fried). Cooking times are given in individual recipes.

The same pan can be used for all types of food and any fat left over can be strained and used again, although fish fat should be kept only for frying fish.

Whole fish need only be rolled in seasoned flour, cornmeal or oatmeal before frying. Sole or flounder fillets may be rolled in seasoned flour and dipped in beaten egg, or simply rolled in flour, then fried in butter.

For even browning, shallow fat should come only halfway up food, like the crab cakes shown here

Deep Fat Frying

This method is quicker than shallow fat frying as food is immersed completely. A coating helps to protect the food from the great heat of the fat and also to prevent the fat from becoming flavored by the food. In this way the fat can be used many times for different dishes.

When cool, strain used fat through cheesecloth into a bowl. Cover when cold; store in a cool place until needed.

Choose a deep, heavy pan (called a fat bath or deep fryer), preferably with a pouring lip, that covers the source of heat, and use a special wire basket to fit (it must be reasonably robust to withstand the high temperatures of the fat). A basket with a fine mesh can also be used with a frying pan or skillet for frying small items like croûtons in shallow fat.

You may find it easier to fry foods coated in a soft batter without using a wire basket as batter tends to stick to mesh.

Suitable fats for deep frying are vegetable or nut oil, lard or shortening, or clarified meat drippings, but it is better not to mix them. Olive oil, butter or margarine cannot be used. Never fill a pan more than one-third full of fat or oil.

Melt the fat or put the oil over moderate heat, then increase the heat until the right cooking temperature is reached (see guide on opposite page). Oil must never be heated above 375°F, and for sunflower oil and some commercially prepared shortenings 360°F is the highest recommended temperature. It is important to remember that oil does not 'haze', as solid fats do, until heated to a much

higher temperature than is required (or safe) for frying.

Apart from food cooked on a rising temperature (e.g. pirozhki) fat or oil should never be below 340°F, as it is essential that the surface of the food is sealed immediately. This means it does not absorb fat and is, therefore, more digestible.

The best way to test temperature is with a fat thermometer. Before using, stand it in a pan of hot water, then dry carefully before placing it in the fat bath. The hot water will warm the glass so that it will not break when put into the hot fat.

If you have no thermometer, drop in a small piece of the food to be cooked (e.g. a raw potato). If the fat or oil is at the right temperature, the food will rise immediately to the surface and bubbles will appear around it. Alternatively, drop in a cube of dry bread, which should turn golden brown in 20 seconds at 375°F; 60 seconds at 360°F.

Coatings

There are three types of coatings: **seasoned flour with beaten egg and dry white breadcrumbs** (for fillets of fish, chops, croquettes, etc.); **fritter batter** (for fillets of fish, sweet and savory fritters); and **pastry** (see future Volume).

For a crisp, golden coating, dry white crumbs are essential, so keep a supply ready for use.

Dry White Crumbs
Cut white bread from a stale loaf into cubes (the crusts can be used for browned crumbs). Reduce to fine crumbs, a little at a time, using a blender at

high speed, or rub the bread through a wire sieve. Spread crumbs thinly on a sheet of paper on a baking sheet, cover with more paper and dry in a warm place for 1–2 days until crisp. Store in an airtight container. For uniformly fine crumbs, sift through a wire strainer.

Browned Crumbs
Bake bread crusts in a slow oven until golden brown, then put through the grinder. Sift and store in an airtight container. Browned crumbs are used for any dish coated with a sauce and browned in the oven (see gratin dishes and cooking 'au gratin' in a future Volume).

Egg and Crumbs
Place a board or plate on your work surface on your right. Sprinkle this well with flour, seasoned with a pinch of salt and a small pinch of pepper. Place some beaten egg on a plate in front of you, and the white crumbs on a large piece of wax paper on the left hand side. Work from your right to your left, as shown in the photographs (preferably using two palette or round-bladed knives to avoid touching with the fingers), beginning by shaping portions on the floured board. After brushing both sides with beaten egg, transfer to the paper of crumbs. Lift corners of paper and tip croquette from side to side to ensure an even coating. Finally, place it on a plate sprinkled with crumbs. The croquette, the name given to this type of crumbed mixture, is then ready for frying.

If convenient, egging and crumbing may be done 1–2 hours ahead.

Lift each shaped portion into beaten egg and brush evenly

Turn over and brush other side; transfer to paper of crumbs

Coat croquette well, pressing on crumbs with a knife

Don't crowd the pan when deep frying; use a clip-on type thermometer

Fritter Batters

Quantities given here for two types of batter are enough to make fruit fritters for 4 people, but large portions of fish need at least half as much again of batter mixture.

Fritter batter 2 is slightly crisper than fritter batter 1.

Fritter Batter 1

$\frac{1}{4}$ cup flour
pinch of salt
2 egg yolks
1 tablespoon melted butter,
    or oil
$\frac{1}{2}$ cup milk
1 egg white

Method
Sift flour with salt into a bowl, make a well in the center and add egg yolks and melted butter or oil. Add milk gradually, mixing to form a smooth batter, and beat thoroughly.

Stand in a cool place (not refrigerator) 30 minutes.

Just before frying, whip egg white until it holds a stiff peak; fold into the batter. Fry in deep fat or fat of $\frac{1}{2}$ inch depth for shallow frying.

Fritter Batter 2

$1\frac{1}{4}$ cups flour
pinch of salt
$\frac{1}{2}$ cake compressed yeast,
    or $\frac{1}{2}$ package dry yeast
1 cup warm water
1 tablespoon oil
1 egg white (optional)

Method
Sift flour and salt into a warm bowl. Sprinkle yeast over half warm water; leave until dissolved, stirring occasionally. Stir into flour with oil. Add remaining water to make a batter the consistency of thick cream. Beat well, cover, leave 15 minutes or until well risen. If using egg white, whip until it holds a stiff peak; fold into the batter just before frying.

Types of Fritters

Fritters — 'beignets' in French: the word is believed to come from the Celtic for 'swelling'.

Soufflé fritters — 'nun's sighs': made from choux pastry; after frying, roll in granulated sugar and serve with a sweet jam or honey sauce. Savory soufflé fritters (to be covered in a future Volume) are often sprinkled with grated Parmesan cheese.

Kromeski: the name given to small pieces of cooked, creamed chicken, veal or game mixture wrapped in thin strips of bacon before dipping in batter and frying.

Almost anything can be turned into a fritter, from cardoons (edible thistles) to brains, tongue and truffles, oysters, rice, candied fruit, squash blossoms or violets. The most common choice is raw fruit, usually apples and bananas.

Apple and Banana Fritters

2–3 tart apples
2 bananas
2 teaspoons lemon juice
fritter batter
deep fat, or about $\frac{1}{2}$ inch
    depth of fat in frying pan
granulated sugar (for sprinkling)

Method
Prepare fritter batter (using recipe 1 or 2); set aside.

Pare and core apples and cut them in $\frac{1}{2}$ inch slices. Peel bananas and cut diagonally in 3–4 pieces. Sprinkle both fruits with lemon juice.

Heat the fat. When it reaches correct temperature (350°F–375°F), coat half of the fruit in batter. Lift from batter with a slotted spoon and slide into the hot fat. Fry fritters until golden brown, drain on paper towels and arrange on a hot platter. Coat and fry remaining fruit and sprinkle with sugar just before serving.

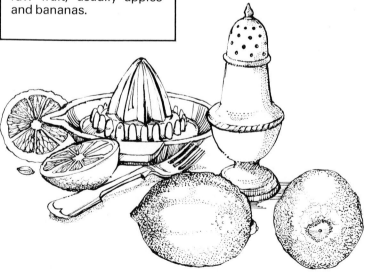

Sprinkle confectioners' sugar over apple and banana fritters before serving

To Fry Fish

Fish such as fillets of sole or flounder, or small whole flounder, are best in an egg and breadcrumb coating. Haddock and perch crumble easily, so fry them in batter.

Fried fish can be garnished with sprigs of fried parsley and a savory butter like maître d'hôtel.

Fish in Batter

Use the second fritter batter recipe (double quantity for ease in working). For white fish like haddock or perch fillet, allow $1\frac{1}{4}$–$1\frac{1}{2}$ lb for four people. Cut into four portions, removing any skin, sprinkle lightly with salt and lemon juice and leave 30 minutes. Drain off liquid, dry fish on paper towels and roll in seasoned flour.

Have batter ready before heating fat. When fat is at 350°F–375°F, lower a piece of fish into batter, turn it to coat thoroughly, lift out with a slotted spoon; lower again, carefully, into fat. Fry about 3 pieces at a time, allowing room to turn them.

When well browned and crisp, lift out and drain well on paper towels. Remove scraps of batter from fat before frying the next batch.

Fish in Egg and Crumbs

Wash fish fillets, dry thoroughly on paper towels and coat by rolling in seasoned flour. Shake to remove surplus flour. Draw through beaten egg, first on one side, then on the other, and gently run down the whole length of the fillet with your finger and thumb to remove any surplus egg. Coat with white crumbs, pressing gently with a knife to cover thoroughly.

When ready to fry, heat fat and place basket in it. When correct temperature is reached (350°F–375°F) take up a fillet and, holding each end between a finger and thumb, twist it. This is done to avoid sogginess when frying in deep fat. It reduces the flat surface of the fish that would normally come in too much contact with the serving dish and with the other fillets. As a result, fillets also look more attractive.

Lower the twisted fillets to the surface of the fat and gently let go; add about three at a time. When fillets are a deep golden brown, lift out basket and stand it on a plate. Leave 1–2 minutes before lifting out fillets onto a hot platter. Scatter with fried parsley; serve sliced maître d'hôtel butter separately.

Fried Parsley
Thoroughly wash and dry a small bunch of parsley and tie with a long string. After frying food, allow fat to cool a little before lowering in parsley. Stand back as it will spit. After 30 seconds, or when spluttering stops, lift out parsley with the string. Discard stems and drain sprigs on paper towels. Serve with most fish and deep-fried foods.

Maître d'Hôtel Butter

$\frac{1}{4}$ cup sweet butter
2 teaspoons chopped parsley
few drops of lemon juice
salt and pepper

Method
With a palette knife, cream butter on a plate; work in parsley, lemon juice and seasonings. Form into a roll, wrap in wax paper and chill. Cut into slices.

French Fried Potatoes

4–6 even-sized potatoes
deep fat
salt

Method
Square off ends and sides of the potatoes, cut into $\frac{1}{2}$ inch thick slices, then into thick sticks. Soak in cold water for about 30 minutes and drain. Wrap in a cloth, or in paper towels, and leave 20–30 minutes. Heat fat and then dip frying basket in it (this prevents potatoes from sticking to it). Lift basket out of fat, put potatoes in; when fat reaches the right temperature (350°F), carefully lower basket into it.

Fry gently until potatoes are just soft (pierce with point of a knife to test) but not colored. Lift out and drain — they can be left like this for a short time before the final frying. Reheat fat to 360°F–375°F. Carefully lower basket of potatoes into fat; fry until a deep golden brown. Drain French fries well on paper towels, turn into a hot serving bowl and sprinkle with salt.

Lower the twisted fish fillet to the surface of the hot fat; let go gently to avoid splashing

Risotto Bolognese with chicken livers, sliced mushrooms, and garnished with chopped parsley (recipe is on page 65)

Cooking with Rice

There are as many ways of cooking rice as there are countries that consume it.

Orientals like their rice moist, so it can be picked up with chopsticks in a sizeable mouthful instead of grain by grain. Persians go to elaborate lengths to dry their rice and then bake it to form a crisp brown crust on the bottom.

According to Western tastes, boiled rice should be tender and fluffy with grains that easily fall apart at the touch of a fork. To achieve this it is important to choose the right kind from the three types of white rice — long grain, medium grain and round grain.

Long grain is best for boiling and is readily available, often parboiled or preprocessed. Medium and round grain rices absorb more liquid than long grain varieties and should be used whenever possible for puddings and pilafs since the extra liquid also adds more richness and flavor.

Glutinous rice, a sweet variety, cooks to a sticky mass which is easily molded to decorative shapes and tastes quite different from regular rice. It is used in Oriental cooking.

In addition to the varieties of white rice, there is brown rice — white rice with only the husk stripped away, leaving the outer layers of the grain. Brown rice is nutritious and full of flavor, and can be substituted for white rice in many recipes, though it takes much longer to cook — 35–40 minutes boiling as compared with 10–12 minutes for white rice.

Wild rice (the seeds of a grass) needs the longest cooking of all and always retains a characteristic chewy texture and nutty flavor.

All methods of cooking rice have the same enemy — starch. The loose particles of cooked starch on the outside of boiled rice must be dried or washed away if the grains are not to coagulate into a sticky mass.

Remember: initial cooking must be fast so the grains are cooked through before outside becomes mushy. Rice must never be overcooked — even 1–2 minutes can make the difference between success and mediocrity. Cooked rice must never be stirred when it is very hot because this breaks the grains into a paste.

Try cooking rice with foods of varying flavors — rice has a knack of blending with other foods.

Boiled Rice

Allow $\frac{1}{4}$ cup rice per person and wash it in a strainer if you wish (this is not necessary for most rice). In a large pan bring plenty of salted water to a boil – at least 3 quarts per cup of rice – and add a slice of lemon to bleach the rice and add flavor.

Add the rice and boil as fast as possible for 10–12 minutes or until the grains are just tender. Rice overcooks easily, so watch the cooking time carefully. Stir occasionally with a fork during cooking to prevent it from sticking.

To stop the rice cooking, tip it quickly into a colander and drain, or pour $\frac{1}{2}$ cup cold water into the pan and then drain. Rinse thoroughly with hot water to wash away any remaining starch, making several draining holes in the rice with the handle of a wooden spoon. Turn onto a large platter; leave in a warm place or in a very low oven to dry for at least 15 minutes before serving. Turn rice from time to time with a fork.

For easy reheating, spoon rice into a well-buttered, shallow ovenproof dish which should be small enough for the rice to fill it amply. Place a sheet of buttered paper or foil on top. Reheat the rice, allowing 20 minutes in a moderate oven (350°F) and serve in the same dish.

If **round grain rice** is not available, use long grain rice instead; but remember that long grain rice will absorb slightly less liquid during cooking.

Jambalaya

$\frac{3}{4}$ lb smoked ham, cut in small pieces
2 tablespoons oil
1 green pepper, cored, seeded and chopped
1 onion, sliced
$\frac{3}{4}$ lb cooked, peeled shrimps
4 tomatoes, peeled, seeded and chopped, or 2 cups canned tomatoes, crushed
2 cups water
1 clove of garlic, crushed
2 teaspoons Worcestershire sauce
$\frac{1}{2}$ teaspoon crushed dried red pepper
salt and pepper
$1\frac{1}{2}$ cups rice
1 tablespoon chopped parsley

The name jambalaya comes from the Spanish *jamon*, meaning ham. The dish always contains ham or pork sausage combined with shrimps or crab, or chicken. Serves 4 as a main course.

Method
In a Dutch oven or flameproof casserole heat the oil and fry the ham, green pepper and onion until they are beginning to brown. Add the shrimps, tomatoes, water, garlic, Worcestershire sauce, red pepper and seasoning and bring to a boil. Stir in the rice, cover and simmer 20 minutes or until all the water is absorbed. Let the jambalaya stand 10 minutes in a warm place, then stir in the parsley, taste for seasoning and serve.

Pilaf

1 cup long grain rice
$\frac{1}{4}$ cup butter
1 onion, thinly sliced or chopped
salt and pepper
pinch of saffron, soaked in 2 tablespoons hot water for 30 minutes
2–$2\frac{1}{2}$ cups stock
5–6 tablespoons grated dry cheese

A pilaf should be dry and fluffy when cooked.

Method
In a shallow saucepan or flameproof casserole, heat 3 tablespoons of the butter, and cook the onion gently until soft. Add the rice and continue cooking gently for 2–3 minutes or until the butter is absorbed and the rice grains are transparent. Season well, pour on the saffron liquid and about threequarters of the stock. Bring to a boil, cover pan and cook in a moderate oven (350°F) for 15 minutes. Add a little more stock if necessary, and cook 5–7 minutes longer, when all the stock should be absorbed and the rice tender.

Dot the surface of the rice with the remaining butter; sprinkle with cheese. Cover and leave in a warm place. Just before serving, stir the rice lightly with a fork; turn into a serving dish.

Shredded ham, cooked chicken, raw chicken livers, etc., can also be added to the pilaf with the onion.

Risotto

The secret of a good risotto is to use round grain rice. The Italians grow a special kind with a short, thick grain. Also, the stock (either veal or chicken) used in risotto must have a good strong flavor. Each kind of risotto takes its name from the town or area in Italy where it originated.

A risotto differs from a pilaf in that it is creamy and spreads apart on the plate when served.

A risotto is best cooked on top of the stove, with the stock added gradually as the rice thickens. This helps the grains to swell and, together with the amount of butter used, gives the right soft, creamy consistency. Grated Parmesan cheese may be stirred into the risotto just before serving or sprinkled over it at the table.

Watchpoint: do not wash rice for a risotto, but pick it over carefully to remove any unhusked grains. When cooked, the rice grains should be nicely firm, not mushy in any way.

Cooked risotto will keep hot for up to 30 minutes if left covered in a warm place.

Risotto Bolognese

1¼ cups round grain rice
¼ cup butter
¾ cup chicken livers
1 small onion, chopped
2 cloves of garlic, chopped
1 cup sliced mushrooms
1 tablespoon tomato purée
salt and pepper
3 cups chicken stock
1–2 tablespoons grated
  Parmesan cheese
chopped parsley (for garnish)

Method

Melt two-thirds of the butter in a shallow pan or flameproof casserole, add livers and sauté them briskly until just colored. Remove livers, add onion and garlic and fry slowly. Slice the livers and reserve.

Add mushrooms to pan and, after a few minutes, the rice; fry 4–5 minutes or until grains are white, then stir in tomato purée. Season, and return livers to pan. Add stock gradually, a third at a time until rice thickens. Cook until grains are barely tender and risotto is creamy. Take pan from heat, dot surface with remaining butter and sprinkle with Parmesan. Cover and leave 5 minutes or until ready to serve. Stir once or twice with a fork, turn into a hot dish and garnish with chopped parsley.

Risotto alla Certosina
(Carthusian Risotto)

1 cup round grain rice
½ lb uncooked shrimps
salt and pepper
few drops of Tabasco
1 small onion, chopped
1 carrot, chopped
2 cloves of garlic, chopped
¼ cup butter
1 tablespoon oil
2½ cups fish stock, or
  equal quantities of bottled
  clam juice and water
1 tablespoon chopped parsley

Method

Simmer shrimps in water that is seasoned with a very little salt, pepper and Tabasco sauce for 3 minutes or until just cooked. Drain, peel and chop shrimps. Reserve meat and simmer crushed shells until the liquid reduces to ½ cup. In a saucepan, lightly brown onion and carrot with garlic in the oil and 3 table-spoons of the butter. Add the strained shellfish liquid; simmer until only a tablespoon of liquid is left. Stir in rice and cook 4–5 minutes or until the rice is white. Add stock gradually, and cook in same way as for risotto Bolognese. Five minutes before end of cooking, stir in shrimps and parsley and remaining butter.

Risotto Milanese

1¼ cups round grain rice
1 marrow bone (optional)
¼ cup butter
1 small onion, finely
  chopped
1 clove of garlic, chopped, or
  crushed
pinch of saffron, soaked in
  2 tablespoons hot water for
  30 minutes (optional)
about 3 cups chicken or
  veal stock
salt and pepper
2–3 tablespoons grated
  Parmesan cheese

The quantity of rice given here will serve 4 people as an appetizer or side dish. Double the recipe for a main course.

Sliced mushrooms (about ½ cup) are sometimes added to this risotto with the onion. For special occasions, use ½ cup white wine in place of the same amount of stock.

Method

Scoop marrow from bone and cut into small pieces. Melt half the butter in a shallow pan or flameproof casserole, add marrow, onion and garlic and fry gently 4–5 minutes. Add rice and continue to fry 4–5 minutes, stirring con-tinuously until all the grains look white.

Add saffron liquid and about a third of the stock. Season and simmer un-covered, stirring occasionally, until the rice thickens, then add another third of stock. Continue cooking until rice thickens again. Add remain-ing stock and cook until the grains are barely tender and the risotto is creamy.

Take pan from heat, dot surface of risotto with re-maining butter and sprinkle with 1–2 tablespoons of Parmesan cheese. Cover rice

and leave 5 minutes or until ready to serve. Stir once or twice with a fork, then turn into a hot serving dish. Avoid using a spoon as this makes the rice mushy.

Note: bone marrow is charac-teristic of a risotto Milanese, but both it and the saffron may be omitted. If more convenient, the marrow bone may be boiled before scoop-ing out the marrow, and this should be added to the risotto towards the end of cooking. In either case, use the bone to make stock.

Kedgeree

1½ cups rice, boiled and
  drained
1 lb finnan haddie, simmered
  in milk until tender
5 hard-cooked eggs, chopped
½ cup heavy cream
¼ cup butter
¼ cup chopped parsley
salt and pepper
1 lemon, thinly sliced (for
  garnish)

Kedgeree is the British version of the Indian rice dish kitchri. For a more luxurious dish, cooked salmon can be substituted for the finnan haddie. Serves 4 as a main course.

Method

Drain the finnan haddie and flake it, discarding the bones. Melt the butter in a flame-proof casserole, add the rice, fish, eggs and cream and cook over medium heat, tossing the mixture with 2 forks, until it is very hot. If the mixture seems dry, add more butter or cream.

Add the parsley, taste for seasoning and pile kedgeree into a hot serving bowl. Arrange halved lemon slices around the edge and serve.

65

Paella Barcelonesa is an unusual and very attractive buffet dish

Paella

Anyone who has visited Spain knows that paella is never the same twice — ingredients varying from place to place, restaurant to restaurant and even from day to day, depending on the fish, meat, fowl and vegetables which happen to be available.

Paella was created as an outdoor dish, cooked over an open fire and eaten by families as they worked in the fields. The prepared ingredients are combined in a special two-handled iron frying pan (a paella pan) and cooked fast for the first few minutes. Then the heat is lowered (or the coals are raked from an open fire) and the dish is simmered, uncovered, for about 20 minutes or until all the liquid is absorbed and the rice is cooked and dry. To prevent the rice from sticking if the pan is thin, you can transfer it to a moderate oven (350°F) once it has come to a boil, instead of cooking on top of the stove.

A large frying pan or skillet can be used instead of the paella pan. Cooked chicken or mussels can be used instead of raw ones, but the flavor will not be as good.

Paella Barcelonesa

1 cup long grain rice
12 soft-shell clams
6 tablespoons olive oil
4 pieces of chicken, cut in half
1 medium onion, chopped
1 tomato, peeled, seeded
    and chopped
½ green pepper, cut in strips
1 clove of garlic, crushed
2 cleaned baby squid, cut in
    pieces (optional)
¼ lb smoked ham, cut in strips,
½ cup sliced Chorizo sausage,
    or pepperoni
½ lb medium shrimps
½ lb flounder, or perch, fillets
    cut into serving pieces
2 cups water
large pinch of saffron
    (soaked in 2–3 tablespoons
    hot water for 30 minutes)
salt and pepper

Method

Scrub clams and soak in cold water for 1 hour to remove the sand. Drain them.

In a paella pan or large skillet, heat oil and sauté chicken pieces gently for 10 minutes, browning it on all sides. Remove the chicken pieces, add onion and fry until transparent. Add tomato and cook until soft. Blanch green pepper in boiling salted water for 1 minute, drain and add to pan with garlic. Cook 2 minutes, stir in rice and cook over medium heat until grains are transparent.

Lay chicken pieces on the rice in the bottom of the pan, put squid on top, then ham, Chorizo sausage or pepperoni, shrimps, fish fillets and finally the clams. Pour on water and saffron liquid.

Season, bring to a boil; boil 3–5 minutes. Turn down heat and simmer, uncovered, for 20 minutes or until the rice is tender and the clams are opened.

Wash clams in cold water; scrub them with a stiff brush to clean the shells

Soak the clams in a bowl of lightly salted water for 1 hour to remove mud from inside the shells

Mud from first soaking is left behind by lifting the clams into a colander to drain before cooking

Paella Catalan

1 cup long grain rice
¼ cup olive oil
4 chicken pieces
1 onion, sliced
1 clove of garlic, chopped or
    crushed
thick slice (¼ lb) cooked
    ham, cut in strips
½ lb firm white fish, cut into
    large cubes
12 large uncooked shrimps
1 red bell pepper, cored,
    seeded and chopped, or 2
    canned pimientos, drained
    and chopped
12 large mussels
1 cup green peas, cooked, or
    small package of frozen peas
large pinch of saffron
    (soaked in 2–3 tablespoons
    hot water for 30 minutes)
2½ cups stock, or water
salt and pepper

Method

Heat oil in a paella pan or skillet, add chicken, fry gently until colored. Take out chicken, add onion and garlic; fry until onion is transparent. Add the ham and rice, and fry, stirring, until the rice is transparent. Take from heat. Peel shrimps.

Have fish, shrimps, pepper or pimiento and mussels ready. Scrub mussels under running water; open ones should be discarded. If using fresh red pepper, dice it and blanch 1 minute in boiling water. Arrange all these ingredients on the rice with the peas and the pieces of chicken — if large, these should be halved. Tuck mussels well down in the pan; lay shrimps on top of rice. Add saffron and its liquid to stock or water and pour over the ingredients. Season, bring rapidly to a boil; boil 3 minutes. Turn down heat; simmer gently, uncovered, for 20 minutes or until the liquid is absorbed and all ingredients are cooked.

COFFEE AND COFFEEPOTS

The origins of coffee are as dark and unfathomable as the steamy black brew. Some trace the name back to Kaffa, a province in southwest Ethiopia. It was here, according to one legend, that a shepherd, noticing the strange antics of his flock, found them feeding on an evergreen bush — the coffee bush. After tasting the berries, he rushed to proclaim their exhilarating effects to the world.

Another tale tells how a Mohammedan mullah chanced upon the insomniac properties of coffee while meditating in the desert. On his return from the wilderness, he expounded to his student dervishes the virtues of this plant, so helpful during the long meditations of the faithful. Its fame spread to Medina and Mecca and the career of coffee began.

All the stories agree on one point — the Arabs first recognized the potentialities of the coffee plant and popularized its use throughout the civilized world.

Today, coffee — valued for its pleasantly invigorating effects and stimulus to conversation — is one of the most popular beverages in the world.

Grown in many tropical regions, its quality and taste vary greatly. While the plains yield the largest production, the finest coffees come from higher elevations — Central America, the highlands of South America and Tanzania.

The flavor of the beans depends both on the region where coffee is grown and on the variety of tree, so that branded coffees, which must have a standard flavor, are a blend of many kinds. Coffee-tasting is an art, for the beans defy all known chemical tests for quality and still are evaluated by special tasters who are trained for years to develop their senses of taste and smell.

Roasting — the coffee merchants' final step — also affects the flavor as it starts releasing the bean's aromatic oil. The process is completed in grinding and brewing. The darker the roast, the sharper the flavor. A breakfast blend, for instance, is lightly toasted, while French or espresso coffee is roasted to a deep, rich brown. Roasting must be done just before coffee is sold or vacuum packed, since beans quickly lose strength once roasted.

From then on, bland and mellow or full-bodied, sharp and strong, the blend you choose can be ground at the store or, better still, milled at home to guarantee freshness. Ground coffee loses its potency within a week, while whole ground beans retain their strength longer (and stay fresh for 1–2 months if kept in the freezer).

Beans should be ground to coarse, medium or fine to match the coffeepot. Despite all the regional variations in preparation, basically there are four methods of brewing: drip or filter, percolator, espresso and vacuum. Most coffeemakers use the same principle, adding water just below boiling point, then permitting water to mix with grounds long enough to extract sufficient caffeine, flavor and strength.

Select your favorite from the coffeemakers described on the following page.

To Make Good Coffee

1 **Start with a clean coffeepot.** Coffee contains oils which form a thin film in the coffeemaker. If it is not removed, this oil quickly turns rancid and contaminates any brew.
2 **Use fresh cold water.** Hot water pipes often have mineral deposits that affect the coffee flavor.
3 **Use freshly ground coffee.** Never keep ground coffee, once opened, more than a week. Grind your own if possible.
4 **Use the full capacity of the coffeemaker.** For smaller quantities use a smaller machine.
5 **Never boil coffee.** This releases the oils and makes the coffee bitter.
6 **Serve coffee at once.** Prolonged heating will also turn coffee bitter. If necessary, keep coffee hot in a water bath over a low flame.
7 **Use the right proportions.** The table below gives average strengths; alter these to suit your taste.

Proportions for Making Coffee

1 coffee cup = 6 fluid oz

Servings	Coffee	Water
2 cups	4 tablespoons	1½ cups
4 cups	8 tablespoons	3 cups
6 cups	12 tablespoons	4½ cups
8 cups	16 tablespoons	6 cups
20 cups	½ pound	1 gallon
40 cups	1 pound	2 gallons

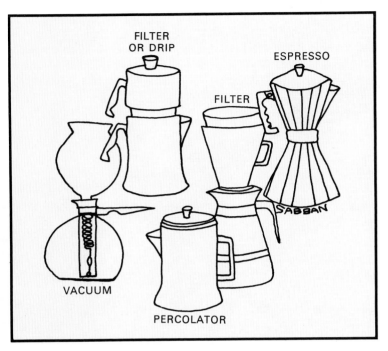

FILTER OR DRIP

ESPRESSO

FILTER

VACUUM

PERCOLATOR

KINDS OF COFFEEMAKERS

Drip or Filter

Most coffee drinkers consider the drip or filter method of brewing coffee to produce the most full-flavored and clearest brew. Water trickling slowly through the coffee grounds extracts the full coffee essence while the filter catches sediments which otherwise might sift into the drink. This method is fast and requires little attention.

The coffeemaker consists of two containers — a jug and a top filter for the coffee grounds. Some have a center basket-strainer usually requiring regular ground coffee, others use filter paper and require finely ground coffee.

Water, boiled and cooled a moment or two, is poured into the top container and left to drip through. The water should be added in 2–3 doses, letting it thoroughly drench the grounds before more is

added. Paper filters are changed for each use.

Metal drip machines of similar design use measured water in the upper section and coffee in the center basket. Hot water drips through the grounds into the lower pot. Metal coffeemakers must be kept scrupulously clean to prevent a metallic taste and, even then, some experts insist that the best coffee can be made only in a glass or ceramic pot.

It is easy to keep coffee warm in most drip and filter machines. Ceramic or earthenware pots can be left on a very low heat or on an asbestos mat over a low heat.

Percolators

Most people use a percolator for making coffee — whether in a five and dime store pot or in the most expensive electric model.

The percolator comes with a jug and basket with attached stem, which holds the regular ground coffee. Water bubbles

up the tube several times over and seeps through coffee.

With non-electric percolators, it is necessary to watch until the desired strength and color is reached, while some automatic percolators can be set for different strengths. Both kinds require little attention and clean easily; however, electrical parts should not be immersed in water.

Non-electric pots can be left on a low heat or on an asbestos mat over a gas flame to keep the coffee warm. Automatics can usually be set at a warming heat once the coffee is made and some are fitted with thermostats to prevent the brew from boiling.

Many sizes of percolator are available, but most have a 6 or 8 cup capacity. Non-electric ones are mostly aluminum, some with chrome finish, stainless steel or flame-proof ceramic glass. Automatic models are available in modern and traditional designs of ceramic or stainless steel.

Vacuum

Vacuum coffeemakers require more attention than other varieties, but many coffee experts swear by this method despite extra work.

The container includes two glass bowls with a center funnel. Finely ground coffee is placed in the top bowl, cold water in the lower, and the machine is put on the heat. When the water boils, the top bowl is inserted into the lower with a slight twist to ensure a tight seal.

Water is forced up through the funnel into the top bowl and gently bubbles through the grounds. A little water should be left below to prevent the vessel from cracking. Stir the water and coffee in the upper bowl briefly, then leave it on a very low heat while the coffee filters back

into the lower bowl, pulled by the force of the vacuum.

These machines are handy for keeping the coffee hot and for making large quantities. Coffee should always be prepared to the full capacity of the coffeemaker, otherwise the bottom container will not hold sufficient water for the process to work. The glass is easy to keep clean but breaks easily. Separate parts, however, can be replaced.

Espresso

The Italian method of brewing coffee produces a strong, sharp flavor and uses the special dark finely ground espresso roast. It is usually served in demitasse cups.

There are two types of espresso coffeemakers. One, the double-tiered Neapolitan type, is an adaptation of the drip method. Cold water is measured in the bottom part, coffee put in the center filter section, the top pot is fitted on with the spout down, then placed on the heat. When the water boils (steam comes down the spout as a signal) the double pot is reversed to let water filter through.

Another version, which comes in both non-electric and automatic models, consists of a one-piece container with center filter basket. Cold water is measured into the bottom part and the coffee basket is screwed into the center. When the water reaches the right temperature, it is forced up at a high pressure through the coffee grounds into the top section.

Non-automatic models must be taken from the heat as soon as the water has risen to keep the coffee from seeping back through the grounds.

Most espresso coffeemakers come in aluminum, but stainless steel and copper varieties are also available.

Give your child a beautiful birthday

Here are delicious ideas for a birthday party your child and guests won't forget. If it's a girl, enchant her with a very unusual birthday cake — a real maypole with colorful streamers that tell each guest where to sit, topped with pretty spring flowers that also decorate the edge of the perfectly iced cake. Or for a boy be different and bake him a numeral birthday cake in the shape of his age; pipe a border of rosettes and put his name on top. Complete the party table with orange baskets, 'mushrooms' of meringue on a field of green gelatine, iced chocolate cookies, and homemade fresh fruit drinks.

Maypole Birthday Cake
or
Numeral Birthday Cake

Field of Mushrooms

Orange Baskets

Iced Chocolate Cookies

Homemade Lemon or Orange Drink

Orange Milk Punch

TIMETABLE

Week before

Make meringues for field of mushrooms and store in airtight container.

Make apricot jam glaze for maypole birthday cake and keep in screwtop jar (or this can be made weeks ahead as it keeps well).

Day before

Make gelatine for field of mushrooms; refrigerate, covered.

Bake chocolate cookies; ice, decorate and store in airtight container.

Make sponge cake and complete maypole birthday cake, store in a safe place away from children, or do not assemble maypole until morning of the party.

Make lemon or orange drink and refrigerate.

Morning of party

Whip cream; complete field of mushrooms. Assemble maypole cake if not done the day before.

Prepare orange baskets and decorate with cream.

Make orange milk punch just before serving.

Field of Mushrooms
(Meringues and Lime Gelatine)

1 package lime gelatine
1 square (1 oz) sweet
   chocolate, grated
1 cup heavy cream

For meringues
2 egg whites
½ cup sugar

Shallow glass bowl; pastry bag; and small plain tube (optional)

Method

Prepare lime gelatine according to package directions. When cool, pour it into the glass bowl and chill until set.

To make meringues: set oven at very low (250°F). Beat egg whites until they hold a stiff peak, and then whisk in 2 teaspoons of the measured sugar for 1 minute only. Fold in remaining sugar quickly with a metal spoon. With a spoon or a pastry bag fitted with the plain tube, shape or pipe a number of small mushroom-shaped caps and stems on a baking sheet lined with silicone paper. Sprinkle the caps lightly with chocolate and bake in heated oven for about 45 minutes. Remove from oven and cool on a wire rack.

Stiffly whip the cream. With a finger or handle of a spoon, gently press in the underside of the 'mushroom caps' and fill the cavities with whipped cream. Sprinkle with grated chocolate and put the stems into the dents. Spread any remaining whipped cream on top of the set gelatine and arrange the mushrooms on top.

Orange Baskets

6–8 large oranges (enough to
   make 2 cups juice)
3–4 lemons
1½ envelopes gelatin
1 cup water
½ cup sugar
rind of 2 oranges, thinly peeled
½ cup sweetened heavy cream
   (to finish) – optional

Pastry bag or paper cone; and small star tube (optional)

Method

With a sharp knife, remove nearly a whole quarter-section from each orange. Leaving a strip wide enough for the handle, remove the other quarter section from the same half. Halve the lemons, scoop out the flesh of these and the oranges, and press it through a strainer, or purée in a blender, and strain to remove the juice. Gently press the orange skins to flatten their bases so the halves sit flat. Sprinkle gelatin over ½ cup cold water to soften.

In a saucepan combine remaining water, sugar, orange rind and soaked gelatin, and stir over a low heat until sugar and gelatin are dissolved. Cover and let stand, off the heat, for 10 minutes. Line a strainer with a piece of damp cheesecloth, pour in the gelatin mixture and combined orange and lemon juice. When liquid has drained through and is cool, pour it into the prepared orange shells; refrigerate until set.

Stiffly whip the cream. If you like, decorate the rims of the baskets with little rosettes of cream, piped through a pastry bag, or paper decorating cone (see page 78) fitted with a small star tube.

Iced Chocolate Cookies

½ cup butter
½ cup sugar
1 egg
1 cup flour
1 teaspoon baking powder
pinch of salt
¼ cup cocoa

For icings
2½ cups confectioners' sugar,
   sifted
½ egg white
pink and blue food coloring

Paper cone and small plain tube

Recipe makes 12 sandwiched cookies.

Method

Set oven at moderately hot (375°F).

In a bowl, cream butter and work in sugar gradually until mixture is light and fluffy; beat in the egg. On a sheet of wax paper sift flour, baking powder, salt and cocoa. Thoroughly blend flour mixture into the butter mixture, and shape dough into small balls the size of a walnut. Place balls quite far apart on a greased baking sheet. Flatten the surface of each with the prongs of a fork dipped often into cold water and bake in heated oven for 8–10 minutes. Remove cookies from the oven and let stand on the baking sheet for several minutes before transferring to a wire rack to cool.

To make the glacé icing: sift just over half of the confectioners' sugar into a bowl and mix to a smooth, stiff paste with water, adding water 1 teaspoon at a time. Stand bowl in a saucepan of hot water and stir gently until the icing thins a little. Coat

cookies with white icing and let stand until the icing is firm.

To make the royal icing: beat egg white lightly with a fork and beat in enough of remaining sifted confectioners' sugar to make a very stiff mixture. Divide in two; tint one half pink, the other blue.

Using a decorating cone and tube, pipe the initials of each child on the surface of the cookies — pink icing for a girl and blue for a boy.

Numeral Birthday Cake

If you have no numeral cake pans you can bake cakes in round, square or oval pans and cut them to appropriate shapes after they have been cooked. For number 3, for example: bake a shallow cake in a large tube pan. Cut the cake in half, remove a wedge-shaped slice from each half and fit the halves together to make a 3.

Method

Make sponge cake as for maypole cake (see page 76) and bake batter in correct numeral pan for the child's age. When cool, place cake on board or tray for icing. Brush well with hot apricot jam glaze and let cake stand until glaze cools. Ice with glacé icing (see maypole cake method). Decorate with child's name and candles.

Maypole Birthday Cake

For sponge cake
¾ cup butter
grated rind and juice of
 1 medium orange
¾ cup sugar
3 eggs, separated
1½ cups self-rising flour
pinch of salt

For apricot jam glaze
5 tablespoons apricot jam
1–2 tablespoons water

For glacé icing
3 cups confectioners' sugar,
 sifted
water

For royal icing (to decorate)
1 egg white
1½–2 cups confectioners'
 sugar, sifted
various food colorings

*8–9 inch springform pan; 6–12
 inches long rod; 1 yard each
 narrow ribbon in four colors;
 few artificial flowers wired
 together in shape of a wreath*

This is a very pretty cake for a child's party. If you like, 1 cup all-purpose flour sifted with 1 teaspoon baking powder may be substituted for 1 cup self-rising flour.

For details on how to pipe decorations and instructions on how to make a piping cone for decorating, see pages 78–79.

Method

Grease and flour the springform pan. Set oven at moderately hot (375°F).

In a bowl cream butter with grated orange rind. Add sugar gradually and beat mixture until light and fluffy. Add egg yolks, one at a time, beating hard after each addition. Sift flour and salt onto a sheet of wax paper. Beat egg whites until they hold a stiff peak. Fold flour and strained juice of half the orange into the creamed mixture; then fold in the egg whites. Pour batter into the prepared pan and bake in heated oven for 30–35 minutes or until the cake springs back when pressed lightly with a fingertip. Cool on a wire rack.

To make the apricot jam glaze: combine apricot jam and water in a pan, warm it over a low heat to melt the jam, pour through a sieve, return to the pan and boil gently until clear. Brush the cake with hot apricot glaze and let stand until set.

Watchpoint: this coating of glaze prevents cake crumbs from spoiling the appearance of the icing when it is poured and spread over the cake.

To make the glacé icing: put sifted confectioners' sugar in a bowl. Stir in the strained juice of the second half of the orange and enough water, adding 1 teaspoon at a time, to make a really thick paste. Warm the icing bowl by standing it in a saucepan of hot water, but take care that the mixture does not get too hot as this will cause the icing to lose its gloss. At all times you must be able to hold the palm of your hand on the bottom of the bowl. When the icing begins to thin to a spreading consistency, pour or spread it over the cake as smoothly as possible.

To make the royal icing: lightly beat or whisk the egg white in a bowl. Beat in the sugar, 1 tablespoon at a time, adding enough so the icing stands in peaks. Divide it into 2–3 batches and tint each batch to different pastel shades with food coloring. Pipe small flowers around the top and bottom edge of the cake and pipe the child's name and age on top, if you like.

To make the maypole: twist the ribbons around and up the rod and secure them with a dab of glue, or tape, at the top, together with the wreath of flowers, letting the ends of the ribbons fall from the wreath. Put the maypole in the center, or to one side, of the cake with the ends of the ribbons leading to name cards on the table.

Birthday Party Drinks

Delight your birthday child and party guests with a fresh **homemade lemon** or **orange drink**: wipe 3 lemons and dice them, unpeeled, into a bowl (try not to lose any juice). Stir in 3 tablespoons sugar and pour on 5 cups boiling water. Let mixture stand for 20–30 minutes until the lemon flavor is strong but not bitter. Strain, chill and stir. Put a sprig of mint into a serving pitcher with ice cubes and 1–2 extra slices of fresh lemon and pour in the lemonade.

To make an **orange drink**: simply squeeze juice from fresh oranges, add sugar if you like, and pour over ice cubes.

Or make up an **orange milk punch**: combine and whisk together $\frac{1}{2}$ cup orange juice, $1\frac{1}{2}$ cups milk and 2 teaspoons sugar. Chill the punch thoroughly and whisk it before serving. This quantity fills 6 punch cups, but the recipe can be multiplied.

HOW TO MAKE A PIPING CONE

Using a Pastry Bag or Paper Decorating Cone

Cream is piped through decorating tubes that are fitted into the end of a pastry bag or paper decorating cone.

Piping fancy decorations of icing, such as names on cakes and cookies, needs more control and generally uses less filling. For elaborate cakes, many different tubes may be needed; it is most economical to make paper cones for decorating instead of using pastry bags. In this way several tubes can be employed at the same time and cones discarded after use.

When holding a decorating bag, either of nylon or paper, the pressure should come from the top with your right hand. Hold your left hand lower down, near the tube, and guide the tube with it. Practice making the decorations and name before you tackle the cake itself.

1 *Fold a 10 inch square of wax or silicone paper; cut into two triangles. With center point up, fold one long edge to meet right-angled point*

2 *Take the other long edge and bring it over and around to the back until all the points of the paper triangle meet at the center back to form a cone or bag*

3 *Fold over the area where all three points of the cone meet. Firmly crease this flap with a fingernail so as to prevent cone from unfolding*

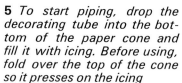 

4 *Snip a little bit off the point of the cone; drop in the decorating tube to see if it fits. If necessary, carefully cut more off the tip so the tube fits tightly*

5 *To start piping, drop the decorating tube into the bottom of the paper cone and fill it with icing. Before using, fold over the top of the cone so it presses on the icing*

PIPING DECORATION

Before starting any decoration, practice the shapes. If you want to decorate a cake with flowers, practice making the centers of flowers by building up a number of small circles, one on top of another

Make a fresh piping cone; this time cut a small 'V' at the point. Practice making petals (without a tube) by pushing icing through the cone onto a firm surface; quickly draw the cone away to make a sharp point

For finished flowers: pipe onto silicone paper first the petals for the outside of each flower, then pipe second row of petals inside. (With experience, flowers can be piped directly onto the cake)

Pipe the centers and leave the completed flowers on the paper until they are dry. Carefully lift the flowers off the paper with the tip of a knife. Attach them to the cake with a dab of icing on the bottom of each flower

To Pipe Colored Flowers

Make 2–2½ cup quantity white royal icing and color about one-eighth of it your chosen color. Fit a medium slanting petal tube into a paper decorating cone. Spread some of the colored icing down the side of the cone to the thin end of the tube opening; lay a knife over this, fill the cone with white royal icing and remove the knife. Fold over the end of the cone to seal it and turn the cone so the thick end of the tube is pointing down.

Attach a 1 inch square of wax paper to a decorating nail (or you can use the round dial on a meat thermometer) with a little icing. Pipe a few circles of icing onto the wax paper to form the flower center.

Pipe 2 more petals onto the flower center, still with the thick end of the tube down. This will form a bud.

To make a medium-sized flower, add 3 more petals. Make about 10 buds and 20 medium flowers for a 9–10 inch cake. For a larger cake, about 14 inches diameter, you will need about 4 times this number if you want to decorate both the top and the sides of the cake with icing flowers.

To make larger flowers: pipe 5 petals onto the medium flowers; let dry for 24 hours before removing paper. You need 5 large flowers for a small cake and 15 for a large one.

Rolled stuffed roast of veal served with gravy and petits pois à la Française (recipe is in Volume 1)

HOW TO ROAST MEAT (2)

VEAL

Good veal from milk-fed calves is easy to recognize by its delicate creamy color and glossy surface. Unfortunately, the best quality, called 'plume de veau', is a rarity usually found only at top quality butchers or in French and Italian specialty stores. Veal of darker color is really baby beef and has neither the tenderness of true veal nor the rich flavor of good beef.

To make carving easier, most cuts of veal are boned, rolled and tied for roasting. They should also be barded, i.e., covered with a thin sheet of pork fat to add richness during cooking. Remove the fat with the string before serving.

The meat must be basted regularly during roasting as it easily becomes dry and tasteless. Favorite ways of adding flavor are to stuff it with a well-seasoned dressing and to baste the meat during cooking with wine or stock. Veal is roasted either until it is well done, or only faintly pink (to taste) when it should be juicy and meltingly tender. A roast of baby veal, surrounded by piles of fresh spring vegetables of different colors is a feast for the eye as well as the palate and is one of the most sought-after party dishes in France.

Before you begin, refer back to the general notes on roasting in Volume 1.

VEAL FOR ROASTING

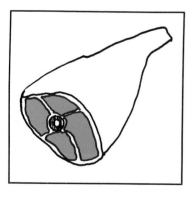

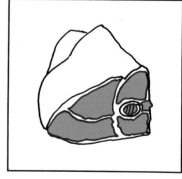

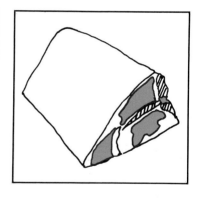

Shank Half of Leg

Leg is the choicest cut, from which escalopes are taken. The leg is normally divided for roasting into the shank half, the center cut and the rump.

Rump

Rump is a triangular cut full of awkward bones; it should always be boned and rolled to avoid difficult carving problems.

Loin

Loin of veal is often cut into chops; it can also be divided into two roasts — loin and sirloin. These cuts dry out easily and should be barded with fat and basted well during cooking.

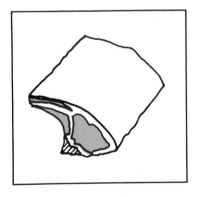

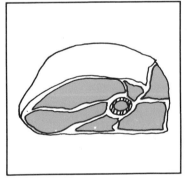

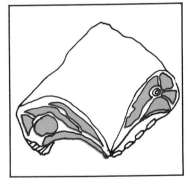

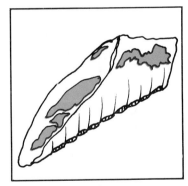

Rib

Rib of veal is often boned and rolled, although it can be left to stand with the bones like a beef rib roast. Crown roast of veal, made like that of lamb from two rib roasts, is a spectacular cut to serve 10–12 people. The center can be stuffed with a dressing, or filled with cooked vegetables just before serving.

Center Cut of Leg

Center cut, which can vary in size from 2–5 lb, has a high proportion of meat to bone and is one of the few veal roasts that is easy to carve when it is left on the bone.

Shoulder

Veal shoulder is good for roasting as sinews and muscles are still tender. It can be boned and rolled, or the blade bone only can be removed, leaving a pocket for stuffing.

Breast

Breast of veal makes an excellent and economical dish. For roasting it should be boned and stuffed — about 3 cups of dressing will be needed to fill an average piece of meat.

ROASTING VEAL

Spread the boned cut of veal with one of the following stuffings, roll it up and tie at 2 inch intervals, or sew it with a trussing needle and string. One cup of stuffing should be enough for an average boneless roast weighing $2\frac{1}{2}$–3 lb (to feed 4 people).

The meat can also be rolled and tied without stuffing. Spread the surface with butter, sprinkle with salt and pepper and set in a roasting pan with $\frac{1}{2}$ cup stock to prevent the meat from drying, or wrap in foil. Roast in a moderately hot oven (375°F), allowing 25 minutes per lb plus 25 minutes more or until a meat thermometer registers 175°F, basting often if cooking in a roasting pan. If cooking in foil, open the package 20 minutes before the end of cooking to allow meat to brown.

Transfer meat to a platter and keep warm. Cook the juices left in the roasting pan (pour those in the foil into pan) until brown and sticky. Stir in 1–2 teaspoons flour and add a cup or more of the stock and stir until boiling and thickened. Then simmer 3 minutes; taste for seasoning and strain.

TO SERVE WITH VEAL ROASTS

Leaf Spinach

$1\frac{1}{2}$–2 lb spinach
3 tablespoons butter
salt and pepper

Method
Wash spinach thoroughly, remove stalks and any thick center ribs. Cook in $\frac{1}{2}$ inch boiling salted water for 5–8 minutes, then drain well in a colander. Press between two plates to squeeze out as much water as possible.

Melt the butter in a saucepan, allow it to brown slightly, then add the spinach and toss over medium heat until dry. Season to taste.

Lima Beans in Sour Cream

3 cups fresh shelled lima beans
2 tablespoons butter
$\frac{1}{2}$ cup sour cream
1 tablespoon chopped chives
salt and pepper

Method
Cook beans in boiling salted water for 15 minutes or until tender. Drain and toss with butter. While still very hot, add sour cream and chives; reheat without boiling. Season to taste.

Potatoes Aurore

10–12 small new potatoes
$\frac{1}{2}$ tablespoon butter

For sauce aurore
1 large ripe tomato, peeled, seeded and chopped, or
1 cup (8 oz) canned tomatoes, crushed
1 clove of garlic, crushed
$\frac{1}{2}$ bay leaf
$\frac{1}{2}$ tablespoon butter
béchamel sauce, made with
3 tablespoons butter,
3 tablespoons flour, 2 cups milk (infused with slice of onion, 6 peppercorns, blade of mace and bay leaf)
1–2 tablespoons heavy cream
salt and pepper

Method
Wash and scrape potatoes, cook them in boiling salted water for 5–6 minutes and drain. Or, if you prefer, boil them in their skins and then peel them.

To make the sauce aurore: in a saucepan combine the tomatoes, garlic, bay leaf and $\frac{1}{2}$ tablespoon butter and simmer until well reduced and pulpy. Work through a sieve or purée in a blender – there should be about $\frac{1}{2}$ cup purée.

Make the béchamel sauce, beat in the tomato purée, add the cream and season to taste.

Add $\frac{1}{2}$ tablespoon butter to the potatoes, pour over the sauce, shake the pan gently to make sure all the potatoes are covered in sauce, add the lid and simmer 6–9 minutes or until the potatoes are tender.

Fondant Potatoes

$1\frac{1}{2}$–2 lb small new potatoes
2–3 tablespoons butter
salt

Method
Scrub or peel potatoes, depending on their age, rinse and dry them. Melt butter in a sauté pan or skillet over moderate heat, add whole potatoes and cover. Shake pan from time to time to turn potatoes; do not lift lid for first 10–15 minutes as steam helps potatoes to cook more quickly, and prevents them from sticking. Prick potatoes with a skewer to see if they are tender; if not, continue cooking a few more minutes. Season with salt and serve in a hot dish.

Caramelized Tomatoes

4 large tomatoes
$\frac{1}{4}$ cup butter
$\frac{1}{4}$ cup sugar
salt and pepper

Method
Halve the tomatoes and place them, cut side up, in a buttered baking dish. Dot with butter and sprinkle with sugar, salt and pepper to taste. Bake in a hot oven (425°F) for 15 minutes or until the tomatoes are just tender and the sugar has caramelized slightly.

Broccoli au Gratin

1 large bunch of broccoli

For sauce
2 tablespoons butter
1 shallot, finely chopped
2 tablespoons flour
1½ cups chicken stock
salt and pepper
2 teaspoons Dijon-style mustard
squeeze of lemon juice
1 egg yolk, mixed with 3 tablespoons heavy cream (for liaison)
¼ cup grated Parmesan cheese

Method
Wash the broccoli, peel the stems with a vegetable peeler to remove the hard outside skin, trim the ends and cut large pieces in half. Cook broccoli in boiling salted water for 8–10 minutes or until just barely tender. Drain, refresh and drain again. Lay cooked broccoli in a buttered heatproof serving dish and keep warm.

To make the sauce: in a pan melt the butter and cook the shallot until just soft but not browned. Stir in the flour and cook over medium heat until pale straw-colored. Take from the heat, pour in the stock and bring to a boil, stirring. Season and simmer 2 minutes.

Take from the heat and stir in the mustard and lemon juice. Stir a little of the hot sauce into the liaison, add this mixture to the remaining sauce and heat, stirring, until it thickens slightly. Cool the sauce a little, then beat in 2 tablespoons of the cheese and taste for seasoning.

Coat broccoli with the sauce, sprinkle with remaining cheese and brown under the broiler.

Carrots with White Wine

10–12 baby carrots
½ cup white wine
3 tablespoons butter
salt and pepper
1½ tablespoons chopped mixed herbs (parsley, mint and thyme)

Method
Scrape the carrots and cook them in boiling salted water for 15–20 minutes or until tender. Drain them. Return them to the pan and pour over the wine while they are still hot. Boil rapidly until the wine is reduced to 2 tablespoons.

Watchpoint: be sure the wine is well reduced almost to a syrup before adding the butter or the carrots will be too moist.

Add the butter to the pan in 2–3 pieces, off the heat, then heat gently, shaking the pan until the butter is melted. Add the seasoning and herbs and transfer the carrots to a hot serving dish.

Herb and Onion Stuffing

For 1¼ cup quantity
1 tablespoon chopped parsley
1 teaspoon mixed herbs (thyme, basil, oregano)
1 medium onion, finely chopped
¼ cup butter
1 cup fresh white breadcrumbs
grated rind and juice of ½ lemon
salt and pepper
little beaten egg

Method
Put onion in a pan, cover with cold water, bring to a boil and cook 5 minutes. Drain and return to the pan with butter. Cover with foil, pressed down well on the onion, and the lid and cook gently for 5 minutes more or until onion is transparent but not colored.

In a bowl combine breadcrumbs, herbs, lemon rind and seasoning and stir in onion and butter. Add lemon juice with enough egg to bind to a soft mixture.

Pecan Stuffing

For 2 cup quantity
½ cup chopped pecans
1 medium onion, finely chopped
2 stalks of celery, finely chopped
¼ cup butter
8 slices of day-old white bread
salt and pepper

Method
Brown onion and celery in butter in a skillet. Pull bread into coarse crumbs, discarding the crusts, and mix with onions, celery and butter. Then add pecans with plenty of salt and pepper.

Rice Stuffing

For 2 cup quantity
½ cup rice
2 tablespoons butter
½ onion, finely chopped
¼ cup pine nuts
¼ cup seedless raisins
1 cup beef, or veal, stock
salt and pepper
1 tablespoon chopped parsley

Method
In a flameproof casserole, heat butter and sauté onion until soft but not colored. Stir in rice and cook until the grains are transparent. Add pine nuts, raisins, stock and salt and pepper to taste. Cover and cook in a moderate oven (350°F) for 20 minutes exactly. Take pan from the oven and let stand 15 minutes before removing the lid. Stir in the parsley with a fork before using.

Loin of lamb Bretonne, stuffed, is garnished with glazed onions and carrots

ROAST MEATS FOR SPECIAL OCCASIONS

Loin of Lamb Bretonne

2–3 lb loin of lamb, boned
2–3 tablespoons meat
  drippings

For stuffing
2 tablespoons chopped onion
2 tablespoons butter
5 tablespoons fresh white
  breadcrumbs
2 tablespoons chopped mixed
  herbs (thyme, rosemary,
  parsley, oregano)
grated rind of 1 orange and
  2 tablespoons orange juice
salt and pepper
beaten egg
seasoned flour (see box)
browned crumbs

For sauce
1 onion, sliced
flour
1½ cups stock (made with lamb
  bones, 1 onion, 1 carrot,
  both sliced, bouquet garni,
  and seasoning) – see
  ballotine of lamb recipe
1–2 tablespoons red currant
  jelly
orange juice

For garnish
1 cup each glazed onions and
  carrots

Method
Make the stock, strain and measure 1½ cups.
To make stuffing: sauté onion in butter until soft but not browned. Add to bread-crumbs with herbs, orange rind and seasoning. Add orange juice and enough egg to make a soft mixture and spread over the inside of the meat. Roll up and tie securely with string. Roll in seasoned flour, brush with beaten egg and roll in browned crumbs.

Heat the meat drippings in a roasting pan, add meat, baste and roast in a mod-erately hot oven (375°F) for 1¼ hours, or until a meat ther-mometer registers 175°F (well-done meat). Take from pan, remove string and keep warm. Pour off fat from roast-ing pan, leaving the meat juices.

To make the sauce: add onion and cook slowly until brown. Sprinkle in a little flour, add stock and red cur-rant jelly, bring to a boil, stir-ring; simmer 3 minutes. Sharpen the sauce with a little orange juice, season and strain.

Carve the meat and arrange on a platter; garnish with glazed onions and carrots. Spoon over a little sauce, and serve the rest separately.

Ballotine of Lamb with Mixed Herbs

1 small shoulder of lamb,
  boned
shoulder bones (for stock)
bouquet garni
salt and pepper
1 tablespoon mixed herbs
  (parsley, sage, thyme,
  marjoram)
3–4 tablespoons butter (for
  roasting)
½ cup white wine
1 teaspoon arrowroot (mixed to
  a paste with water – optional)

For stuffing
¼ cup butter
1 small onion, finely chopped
1 cup (¼ lb) chopped
  mushrooms
2 tablespoons fresh white
  breadcrumbs
½ cup (¼ lb) finely chopped
  cooked ham
½ cup (¼ lb) finely chopped
  fresh pork
½ cup (¼ lb) finely chopped
  fresh veal
salt and pepper

Method
To make the stock: simmer shoulder bones with the bou-quet garni, salt and pepper in water to cover for 1 hour or more. Strain.

To make the stuffing: melt butter in a pan, add onion and cook until soft but not browned. Add mushrooms and cook 3 minutes. Combine this mixture with breadcrumbs and chopped meats in a bowl and season well.

Open the boned lamb shoulder, sprinkle with mixed herbs and spread with the prepared stuffing. Roll up and tie securely with string. Spread surface of the meat with butter, set in a roasting pan and pour the wine around. Roast 1½ hours in a moder-ately hot oven (375°F) or until meat thermometer registers 175°F (for well-done meat). Baste often during cooking.

Take out the meat and keep warm. Pour off fat from pan, leaving the meat juices, and deglaze with 1½ cups stock from the bones. Season, thicken with the arrowroot paste, if you wish, and strain. Cut the strings from the meat, carve and arrange slices on a platter. Spoon over a little gravy and serve the rest separately.

> For **seasoned flour:** add 1 teaspoon salt and ½ teaspoon pepper to 1 cup flour and mix well. Use for coating fried foods.

Glazed Onions

Cover 18 small onions, peeled, with cold water, add salt and bring to a boil. Drain off the water, add 2–3 tablespoons butter and sprinkle 1 tablespoon sugar over the onions. Cover and cook gently, shaking the pan occasionally until the onions are tender and golden brown with caramelized sugar – this takes about 10 minutes.

Glazed Carrots

Peel 1–1½ lb carrots and quarter them or leave them whole if small. If very large, cut in thin slices. Put in a saucepan with water to cover, 1 teaspoon sugar, 2 table-spoons butter and a pinch of salt. Cover and simmer until tender, then remove the lid and boil until all the water has evaporated – the butter and sugar forms a shiny glaze over the carrots. Just before serving, sprinkle with chopped mint.

Leg of Lamb Duxelles

1 small leg of lamb
5–6 tablespoons butter
1 clove of garlic, peeled and cut in slivers
$\frac{1}{2}$ cup white wine
$\frac{1}{2}$ cup stock
1 teaspoon arrowroot (mixed to a paste with 1 tablespoon water – optional)
3–4 tablespoons grated Parmesan cheese
watercress (for garnish)

For duxelles filling
2–3 cups ($\frac{1}{2}$–$\frac{3}{4}$ lb) chopped mushrooms
2 tablespoons butter
2 shallots, or scallions, finely chopped
2 teaspoons thyme
1 tablespoon chopped parsley
3 tablespoons fresh white breadcrumbs
salt and pepper

Method

Spread meat with 2 tablespoons butter; with a small pointed knife, make several incisions and slip into these the garlic slivers. Wrap lamb in buttered foil, place in a roasting pan and cook in a moderate oven (350°F) for $1\frac{1}{2}$ hours, or until meat thermometer registers 175°F (for well-done meat). Halfway through cooking, remove foil, pour over most of the wine and baste often during remaining cooking time.

To make the filling: in a skillet or frying pan, melt butter, add shallots, and, 1 minute later, the mushrooms. Stir in herbs, and cook briskly for 5–6 minutes or until mixture becomes dry. Remove from heat and add breadcrumbs and seasoning.

Take meat from pan and cool slightly. Pour off fat and strain juice into a saucepan. Deglaze roasting pan with stock and remaining wine, strain into the saucepan and season. Thicken this gravy, if you like, with a little arrowroot paste.

Slice lamb and spread each slice with a little duxelles filling. Reshape leg and return to roasting pan. Cream remaining butter with cheese and spread over surface of meat. Brown in a hot oven (425°F) for 10 minutes.

Serve on a hot platter with a little of the gravy spooned around and remainder served separately. Garnish with watercress.

If you slice only the top part of the leg, there should be enough meat left on the underside to make a good 'rechauffé' (dish made from leftover cooked food) on the following day.

> **Duxelles** is a finely chopped mixture of mushrooms, shallots and herbs, cooked in butter and used to flavor soups, sauces and stuffings. The name probably originated in the 17th century with La Varenne, a famous chef, who was an official member of the household of the Marquis d'Uxelles.

Roast Beef Paysanne

$2\frac{1}{2}$–3 lb boned rump of beef
2 tablespoons butter, softened
2 teaspoons Dijon-style mustard
$\frac{1}{2}$ teaspoon salt
$\frac{1}{2}$ teaspoon black pepper, freshly ground
4–5 medium potatoes, cubed
4–5 medium tomatoes, halved
oil (for brushing)
bunch of watercress (for garnish)

For stuffing
$\frac{1}{4}$ lb ham, ground
1 onion, finely chopped
2 tablespoons butter
2 cups fresh white breadcrumbs
1 teaspoon thyme
1 tablespoon chopped parsley
1 egg, beaten to mix
1–2 tablespoons milk (optional)

Method

To make stuffing: fry the onion in the butter until soft. Stir in the ham, breadcrumbs, thyme, parsley plenty of pepper and a little salt. Stir in the beaten egg to bind the mixture, adding a little milk if the stuffing is dry. Fill the stuffing into the cavity left by the bone, enlarging it with a knife if necessary to form a pocket. Reserve any extra stuffing.

Beat the softened butter with the mustard, salt and black pepper until it is smooth and spread this mixture on top of the beef. Set the beef in a roasting pan and cook it in a moderately hot oven (375°F), basting often, for 1 hour or until a meat thermometer inserted in the thickest part of the meat registers 140°F (for rare beef).

Mix the remaining stuffing with the potatoes in a baking dish. Forty minutes before the end of cooking, sprinkle 2 tablespoons pan juices over the potatoes and bake them in the oven with the beef until tender and browned.

Brush tomatoes with the oil, sprinkle with salt and pepper and bake them in the oven with the meat for 10–15 minutes or until tender, or broil them.

Set the beef on a platter, arrange tomatoes around it and pile the potatoes at each end. Garnish with watercress.

Contrefilet Dubarry

2–3 lb top end of beef rib, boned, well-trimmed and rolled
2–3 tablespoons meat drippings, or oil (for roasting)
$1\frac{1}{2}$ cups beef stock and a little flour (for gravy)

For thick mornay sauce
2 tablespoons butter
2 tablespoons flour
$1\frac{1}{4}$ cups milk
salt and pepper
$\frac{1}{4}$ cup grated cheese
1 large cauliflower (for garnish)

Dubarry is the name given to any recipe with cauliflower as a garnish or in a sauce.

Method

The garnish for this dish can be prepared ahead and baked later with the meat. Divide the cauliflower into sprigs and boil in salted water for 7 minutes or until just tender. Drain and refresh under cold running water. Take 2–3 sprigs at a time and squeeze lightly together in a piece of cheesecloth and set on a buttered baking sheet.

To prepare mornay sauce:

melt butter in a saucepan; when foaming, remove from heat and stir in flour. Add one-third of the milk; blend well before adding the rest. Season lightly, return to heat, stir until boiling. Boil 1—2 minutes. Gradually beat in the cheese, reserving a little.

Coat each 'bouquet' of cauliflower with sauce and sprinkle with the reserved cheese. To serve, reheat in a moderately hot oven (375°F) for 20 minutes or until golden brown.

Set oven at hot (400°F). In a roasting pan heat the drippings or oil; when sizzling, add meat, baste with fat, turn and baste again. Roast for 1—1¼ hours in heated oven or until a meat thermometer registers 170°F (for well-done meat). Baste often during cooking. Prepare gravy, using the beef stock.

Arrange the cauliflower bouquets around the meat on a platter; serve gravy and roast potatoes separately.

Larding and Barding

Larding (see photograph above) means the insertion of small strips of fresh pork fat or bacon into the flesh of meat which has very little natural fat. This prevents meats such as fillet of beef, veal, venison and guinea hen from drying out when roasted. The fat used must be white, firm and dry, and cut into pieces about ¼ inch wide and 1½ inches long. It is threaded into a larding needle — a large needle with a channel to enclose the fat, or with a spring at the end to catch the fat so it can be pulled through the meat. The strip is literally 'sewn' into the meat, leaving both ends hanging over the surface. Larding is always done across the grain of the meat, as above. The fat should be chilled before it is cut into strips.

Barding means covering the breast of a bird or a piece of veal or venison with thin sheets of fat before roasting. Like larding, this prevents the flesh from drying out during cooking. The fat is usually tied around with string. Barding can be done with strips of bacon or with thin even slices of pork fat.

Loin of Pork Alsacienne

2½—3 lb loin of pork
1½ cups stock (see below)
1 onion, sliced
1 carrot, sliced
bouquet garni
1 teaspoon oil
salt and pepper
2—3 tablespoons meat drippings
fresh white breadcrumbs
1 tablespoon flour

For cabbage mixture
1 small green cabbage, shredded
2 tablespoons butter
1 onion, finely sliced
1 lemon, peeled and sliced
salt and pepper
4 dessert apples

For garnish
1 tablespoon chopped parsley
2 hard-cooked eggs, quartered

Method

First prepare stock: in a heavy pan put chine bone, onion and carrot with oil and brown over medium heat. Cover with cold water, add bouquet garni, season and simmer, covered, for at least 1 hour. Strain.

Heat drippings in roasting pan. Add meat and baste well with hot drippings. Roast in a moderately hot oven (375°F) for 1½ hours, or until meat thermometer registers 170°F. Cover fat of meat with breadcrumbs 20 minutes before end of cooking, baste well and return to oven to brown.

To make cabbage mixture: blanch the cabbage in boiling salted water for 1 minute, then drain and refresh under cold running water; set aside. In a flameproof casserole, melt butter, add onion and cook slowly until soft but not browned, then mix into cab-bage, add lemon slices and seasoning. Pare, quarter and core apples and arrange, rounded side down, at bottom of the casserole. Spoon cabbage mixture on top, cover with buttered foil and the lid. Cook gently on top of stove for 15—20 minutes; continue cooking 30—40 minutes in oven with pork.

Take out meat and keep warm. Pour off fat from pan, leaving juices, stir in flour and cook until brown. Pour on 1½ cups stock, season, bring to a boil, stirring; cook 3 minutes. Strain. Slice meat, arrange on a hot platter and spoon over the gravy.

Run a palette knife around the inside of casserole and turn cabbage onto a hot dish — it should fall out like a cake. Sprinkle parsley on top and surround with egg quarters.

Petits pots de crème, arranged on a platter, are attractive desserts for a buffet (recipe is on page 95)

HOW TO MAKE CUSTARDS

Custards play an important part in both simple and sophisticated dishes. They form the basis of quiches and vegetable custards and of many desserts. Vanilla custard sauce is a favorite accompaniment for sweet soufflés and fruit dishes. The basic ingredients of custards are eggs and milk used in varying proportions, with different flavorings according to the recipe.

There are two kinds of custards. For the first, eggs and milk are mixed together and baked or steamed until firmly set, as for crème caramel. In the second type, yolks and milk are cooked over gentle heat to a creamy consistency. This softer custard is the basis of cold sweet mousses and soufflés set with gelatin.

Points to remember

1 Egg whites set a custard and egg yolks give it a creamy consistency. For a custard which is baked or steamed, the proportions should be 1 egg plus 1 yolk to 1 cup of milk; for a soft custard, use 2 egg yolks to 1 cup of milk. For richness, more egg yolks may be added to either kind of custard or, for economy, 1 teaspoon of cornstarch can be used instead of an egg yolk.
2 Egg yolks and milk will curdle if they are cooked too fast or over too high a heat. When whites are included, these make a mixture curdle even more easily.
3 Use a water bath when baking a custard in the oven. A soft custard can be made in a double boiler but, with care, the custard can be thickened over direct gentle heat. The milk should always be scalded before adding it to the eggs.

Cooking in a Water Bath

This term applies to a method of cooking delicate mixtures (custards, creams, etc.) in the oven, as opposed to keeping sauces, etc. hot in a water bath or double boiler on top of the stove.

A large pan, such as a roasting pan, is half filled with hot water and the dish or mold is placed in the center. The pan, with its contents, is then cooked in the oven for the given time. The water protects the mixture from direct oven heat which might cause curdling. During cooking, cover the dish in the water bath with foil unless you want the top of the custard or cream to be browned.

Custard Pudding

2 cups milk
strip of lemon rind (optional)
2 eggs
2 egg yolks
1½ tablespoons sugar
½ teaspoon vanilla (optional)
½ tablespoon butter
pinch of grated nutmeg (optional)

Baking dish (3 cup capacity)

Method
Butter the dish. Scald milk with lemon rind, if used. Beat eggs and yolks until mixed, but not foamy, and blend in the sugar with vanilla, if used. Stir in scalded milk gradually and strain custard into the baking dish. Dot the surface with butter and sprinkle with nutmeg.

Stand the dish in a water bath and cook in a moderate oven (350°F) for 35 minutes or until a knife inserted near the center of the custard comes out clean and the top is brown. Serve hot or cold.

Custard Pie

For rich pie pastry
1½ cups flour
¼ teaspoon salt
½ cup butter
1 tablespoon sugar
1 egg yolk
2 tablespoons water

For custard filling
4 eggs
2 tablespoons sugar
2¼ cups milk, scalded
½ teaspoon vanilla
¼ teaspoon grated nutmeg

7–8 inch springform pan, or small deep molds

This should be made in a deep pie pan or deep individual molds so a good proportion of custard goes with the pastry.

Method
Prepare the pastry dough and chill. Roll out dough and line the pie pan or molds, prick the bases very lightly, set on a baking sheet and chill again.

In a bowl, mix the eggs lightly with a fork, add sugar, scalded milk and vanilla. Cool mixture and strain into the pastry shells, filling them to about ¼ inch from the top. Sprinkle with nutmeg.

Set oven at hot (425°F) and put in a second baking sheet to heat. When very hot, put the first baking sheet with the pie or molds directly on top of the already heated sheet. This heats the baking sheet quickly and helps bake the bottom of the pastry.

Bake in heated oven for 15 minutes for the pie, or 8 minutes for the small molds. Then reduce heat to 350°F and bake a further 15 minutes for both pie and molds or until a knife inserted near the center of the custard comes out clean.

Cool and remove the pie from the pan, or turn out from the molds. Serve cold.

Vanilla bean gives a particularly delicate flavor to custard or cream. The beans are comparatively expensive, but they can be used several times if washed and dried between uses. Little white crystals on the bean indicate its freshness.

The seeds hold most of the flavor; therefore, it is best to split the bean and scrape out some of the tiny black seeds to use with it. Once used, rinse the bean in warm water and allow to dry before storing in a small jar of granulated sugar. Keep well sealed. This **vanilla sugar** may be used for flavoring cakes and custards.

Crème à la Vanille
(Vanilla Custard Sauce)

1 cup milk, or half and half
1½ tablespoons sugar
½ teaspoon vanilla, or
½ vanilla bean, split
2 egg yolks

Method
Put milk in a pan with the sugar. If using a vanilla bean, infuse it in the milk for 10 minutes, keeping the pan covered, take out the bean, then add the sugar.

Beat egg yolks in a bowl until lightly colored, scald the milk and gradually stir into the yolks, with the vanilla, if using. Return to pan and stir with a wooden spoon over gentle heat. When the custard coats the back of the spoon and looks creamy, strain back into the bowl. Sprinkle with a little sugar and cool. This coating of sugar melts and helps to prevent a skin from forming.

Watchpoint: if the custard gets too hot and starts to curdle, pour it at once into the bowl without straining and whisk briskly for 10 seconds. Remember that cooking on a gentle heat helps to prevent a custard from curdling and makes it creamier.

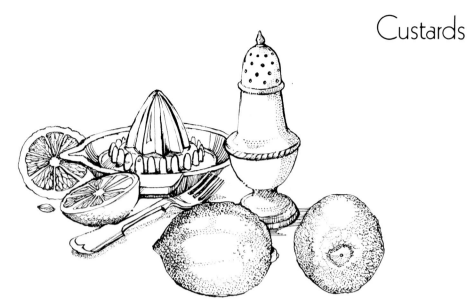

For crème caramel, strain the cool custard mixture into the caramel-coated soufflé dish

Crème Caramel
(Caramel Cream)

2 cups milk
2 eggs
2–3 egg yolks
1½ tablespoons sugar

For caramel
½ cup cube, or granulated, sugar
½ cup water

Soufflé dish, or heatproof mold (3 cup capacity)

Method
Scald milk. Beat eggs and yolks with a fork to mix, but do not allow them to become foamy. A third yolk produces a more creamy result. Stir in the sugar and gradually pour in the scalded milk. Set aside.

To make caramel: dissolve sugar in water over gentle heat, bring to a boil and boil rapidly without stirring until the syrup is a rich brown. Stop it from cooking by dipping base of the pan into a bowl of cold water; when no longer bubbling, pour three-quarters of the caramel into the dry, warm soufflé dish or mold. Immediately turn the dish around carefully to coat the bottom and sides evenly with caramel. Pour the remaining caramel onto a baking sheet.

Strain the custard mixture into the dish, cover with foil and cook in a water bath in a moderately hot oven (375°F) for 40–50 minutes or until a knife inserted near the center comes out clean. Cool. Turn out onto a dish just before serving; crush the remaining caramel and scatter around the molded crème.

Watchpoint: you can lessen the amount of caramel usually left in the mold after turning out by adding 1 tablespoon boiling water to the caramel before pouring it into the dish.

Petits pots de crème can be made in a variety of flavors

Petits Pots de Crème
(Small Pots of Cream)

3 cups milk
vanilla bean
3 eggs
3 egg yolks
1 tablespoon vanilla sugar
   (see page 92), or
   1 tablespoon sugar and
   ½ teaspoon vanilla
2 tablespoons granulated
   sugar
1½ teaspoons dry instant
   coffee
1½ squares (1½ oz) semisweet
   chocolate

*Deep mousse pots, or ramekin
dishes*

For this dessert, use the special deep mousse pots which are made of heatproof china, or ramekin dishes (miniature soufflé dishes). These 'petits pots' look attractive arranged on a large platter on a buffet table. Fill them with a variety of flavors as below.

Method
Heat milk with vanilla bean. Take from heat and leave to infuse, covered, 5–10 minutes until well flavored.

For **vanilla flavored cream**: beat 1 egg and 1 egg yolk with vanilla sugar until mixed but not foamy. Remove vanilla bean from milk and pour 1 cup onto the eggs and sugar. Blend well and strain into pots.

For **coffee flavored cream**: beat 1 egg, 1 egg yolk and 1 tablespoon granulated sugar together. Warm remaining infused milk slightly and stir 1 cup into eggs and sugar. Add coffee, stir until completely dissolved and strain into pots.

For **chocolate flavored cream**: combine remaining egg, egg yolk and granulated sugar. Melt chocolate on a heatproof plate over a pan of boiling water. Add remaining warm, infused milk to eggs and sugar, stir in chocolate and strain into pots.

Place the filled pots in a water bath, cover them with their lids or with buttered foil and bake in a moderate oven (350°F) for 20 minutes or until just set. Take out and chill. Serve plain or with whipped cream.

Bavarois à la Crème
(Bavarian Cream)

3 egg yolks
2 tablespoons sugar
1 vanilla bean, or ½
   teaspoon vanilla extract
2 cups milk
1 envelope gelatin
¼ cup water
1 cup heavy cream

*Plain mold (1 quart capacity);
pastry bag and star tube
optional)*

Method
Beat yolks and sugar in a bowl until creamy and light. Infuse vanilla bean in milk over low heat until well flavored, or add vanilla extract to egg mixture. Stir in scalded milk gradually, first removing vanilla bean, and return to pan. Stir constantly over gentle heat until the custard coats the back of a wooden spoon. Strain into a bowl to cool.

In a small pan, sprinkle gelatin over water and let stand 5 minutes until spongy. Dissolve over a pan of hot water, stirring occasionally. When dissolved, pour into the cooled custard. Transfer custard to a metal bowl or thin pan, set over a bowl of ice (this will help the custard to cool quicker), and stir until the mixture starts to thicken.

Whip cream until it holds a soft shape and carefully fold ¼ cup into the custard. Refrigerate the remaining cream. Turn the custard into a lightly oiled mold and chill.

When firmly set, turn out custard carefully and coat with remaining cream or decorate, if you like, with rosettes of cream piped with a pastry bag fitted with a star tube.

For a **coffee bavarois**: add 1 tablespoon dry instant coffee to the milk while bringing it to scalding point, then pour onto the yolks.

For a **chocolate bavarois**: melt 4 squares (4 oz) semisweet chocolate in the milk before adding to the egg yolks.

For a party dessert for 6–8 people, make two batches of cream, flavoring one with **vanilla** and the other with **chocolate** or **coffee**. Pour vanilla into a large plain cake pan and, when about to set, pour in chocolate or coffee. Gently stir to marble the colors, and chill. When set, turn out and decorate the edge with whipped cream.

> **Gelatin** quantities given throughout are for regular powdered gelatin.
>
> **All custards made with gelatin** should be eaten the day they are made because the consistency tends to toughen if kept for any length of time. Consistency is also better if the mold is served at room temperature, not chilled.

Tangerine Cream

3 tangerines
6–8 cubes sugar
2 cups milk
3 egg yolks
1 tablespoon granulated sugar
1 envelope gelatin
¼ cup cold water
¾ cup heavy cream
1 egg white
2–3 tablespoons red currant
   jelly

*Glass serving bowl (1½ quart
capacity)*

Method
Rub sugar cubes over the rind of the washed tangerines to remove the zest (fruit oil). When soaked with zest, add cubes to the milk and dissolve over gentle heat. Beat yolks with granulated sugar until creamy and light. Stir in scalded milk, return to pan and stir over gentle heat until the custard thickens and coats the back of a wooden spoon. Do not boil. Strain and cool. In a small pan, sprinkle gelatin over the water and stand 5 minutes or until spongy. Dissolve over a pan of hot water and stir into the custard. Transfer to a metal bowl or pan placed over a pan of ice and stir until the custard starts to set.

Stiffly whip cream. Whip egg white until it holds a stiff peak. Fold it carefully into the cream, and then into the custard when it is beginning to thicken. Pour into a glass bowl and chill until set.

Peel and slice tangerines. Dissolve red currant jelly over gentle heat and strain or beat until smooth. Cool. Arrange the slices of tangerine over the cream and, just before serving, coat them with red currant jelly syrup.

Fried or broiled chicken with corn fritters is served with green salad with pineapple (recipe is on page 100)

DINNER WITH A DIFFERENCE

Each dish in this menu makes the simple into something special. To begin, there is fresh asparagus served with a rich Hollandaise sauce, or avocado soup. Familiar fried chicken is garnished with a salad of fresh pineapple for the entrée, and caramel and vanilla custards marbleize the molded gelatin dessert.

For chicken served in this way, you could hardly do better than try one of the beautifully fragrant, delicately sweet white wines from Germany's picturesque Mosel valley. California offers a good alternative, however, with its similarly charming wine from the same grape — Johannisberg Riesling.

Asparagus with Hollandaise Sauce
or
Avocado Soup

Fried or Broiled Chicken
with Corn Fritters
Green Salad with Fresh Pineapple

Caramel & Vanilla Bavarois

∾

White wine – Piesporter (Mosel)
or
Johannisberg Riesling (California)

TIMETABLE

Morning

Prepare both custards for bavarois and let them cool. Make breadcrumbs for fritters and for coating chicken.

If whole, cut chickens into pieces. Trim pieces neatly. Make stock from the trimmings and giblets.

Cook fresh or frozen corn, or drain canned corn.

Wash and trim asparagus. Tie in bunches and stand in cold water.

Prepare avocado soup and liaison but do not mix. Cover soup and liaison with plastic wrap.

Wash lettuce, wrap in dish towel and refrigerate.

Cut pineapple and sprinkle with sugar and refrigerate for at least 30 minutes. Make vinaigrette dressing and pour a little onto pineapple. Chop parsley and keep in small bowl covered with plastic wrap.

Add gelatin to both custards for bavarois, cool and fold whipped cream into caramel and vanilla custards and put mixtures into cake pan when they begin to set. Cover with foil or plastic wrap and refrigerate. Make caramel decoration and sauce.

Coat chicken pieces with egg and breadcrumbs. Cover, but leave at room temperature.

Assemble equipment for final cooking from 6:15 for dinner around 8:00 p.m.

Order of Work

6:15

Remove bavarois from pan and decorate.

Make sauce for chicken and keep warm in a double boiler or set over hot water. Prepare corn fritter mixture. Make Hollandaise sauce and set bowl over warm water to keep warm (it must not get too hot).

7:00

Set oven at low (250°F). Put plates and dishes to warm. Fry fritters, leave them on paper towels near the bottom of the oven. Start frying or broiling chicken.

7:30

Cook asparagus, drain and keep warm. *Heat soup, add liaison and keep hot on an asbestos mat — it should be hot but never come to a boil.*

Fry or broil the bacon, arrange chicken on a platter and garnish with bacon and corn fritters. Keep hot. Mix vinaigrette dressing and toss salad.

8:00

Serve appetizer.

You will find that **cooking times** given in the individual recipes for these dishes have sometimes been adapted in the timetable to help you when cooking and serving this menu as a party meal.

Asparagus with Hollandaise Sauce

2 lb asparagus
1 cup Hollandaise sauce
(see page 51)

Method

Trim the bottom of the asparagus stalks, leaving about 2—3 inches before the green starts. Try to trim so all the stalks are the same length. Rinse them in cold water and, with a vegetable peeler, peel the tough white skin from each stem. Tie the stalks in little bundles with soft cord and, if they are not to be cooked immediately, stand them stalk end down in a bowl of cold water until needed.

Make the Hollandaise sauce.

Stand bunches of asparagus in an asparagus cooker, or in a deep saucepan filled with plenty of boiling salted water, stalk end down and green tips above the water. Cover and cook gently for 10—12 minutes or until the green part is tender. Carefully lift the stalks from the pan, drain them on a clean dish towel, then place them on a folded white napkin on a hot dish. Cut and remove strings. Serve Hollandaise sauce in a separate sauce boat.

Alternative appetizer

Avocado Soup

2 avocados
2½ tablespoons butter
1 tablespoon flour
4 cups jellied chicken stock
1 shallot, or scallion, finely chopped
1 stalk of celery, chopped
salt and pepper
pinch of nutmeg

For liaison
2 egg yolks
2—3 tablespoons heavy cream

Method

Melt butter, stir in flour until smooth, and cook over a low heat until straw-colored. Pour in stock, add shallot or scallion, celery and seasonings. Cook, stirring constantly, until the soup boils. Cover, simmer 10—15 minutes and strain.

Peel avocados and remove the seeds. Mash the flesh with a fork, then work it through a strainer or purée in a blender with a little of the soup. Stir a small quantity of hot soup into the avocado purée, then gradually pour purée into remaining soup, stirring constantly. Mix until smooth and bring to a boil.

Mix egg yolks and cream in a bowl with a wooden spoon, stir in some of the hot soup, then add this gradually to the bulk of the soup. Cook carefully, without boiling, until the mixture thickens. Taste for seasoning, add a pinch of nutmeg and serve.

Serve a rich and creamy Hollandaise sauce spooned over the tender spears of asparagus

Entrée

Fried or Broiled Chicken with Corn Fritters

2 frying chickens (2½–3 lb
  each), or 6–8 breast and
  wing parts
2 tablespoons seasoned flour
1 egg, beaten to mix
1 tablespoon oil
1 cup fresh white breadcrumbs
½ cup butter, preferably
  clarified (see Glossary)
8 slices of bacon (for garnish)

For corn fritters
1 cup cooked fresh or frozen,
  or canned, corn kernels
2 eggs, separated
salt and pepper
pinch of sugar
1 teaspoon baking powder
½–1 cup fresh white
  breadcrumbs
oil (for frying)

For sauce
2 tablespoons butter
1 tablespoon flour
1 cup chicken stock
salt and pepper
1 teaspoon grated fresh
  horseradish, or 1 tablespoon
  prepared horseradish
squeeze of lemon juice
5 tablespoons light cream

Method

If whole chickens are used, cut them into pieces and trim neatly. Roll the pieces in seasoned flour and brush with egg and oil beaten together. Roll in breadcrumbs, pressing crumbs on firmly with a metal spatula.

Watchpoint: when the oil is added to beaten egg before egging and crumbling chicken, the meat retains more moisture.

To make corn fritters: beat egg yolks thoroughly with salt, pepper, sugar and well-drained corn kernels. Beat egg whites until they hold a stiff peak; fold into corn mixture with baking powder and enough breadcrumbs to give a consistency that can be dropped from a spoon.

Put ¼ inch of oil into a skillet and heat. Drop in the fritter mixture, 1 tablespoon at a time; fry until golden brown. Stand back as the fritters may pop. Turn and fry on the other side. Remove fritters from pan with a slotted spoon and drain them on paper towels in a warm oven.

To make the sauce: melt butter in a saucepan, stir in flour until smooth and cook over a low heat until straw-colored. Remove from heat, stir in stock and season with salt and pepper. Cook gently, stirring constantly, until sauce boils. Continue simmering 2–3 minutes, then add horseradish, lemon juice and cream. Keep warm.

To fry the chicken: heat clarified butter in a large skillet, add chicken pieces and cook over a low heat for about 20 minutes, turning occasionally so they are tender and browned evenly on all sides.

To broil the chicken: baste the pieces with heated clarified butter before and during broiling and turn frequently. When they are rich brown in color and tender when tested with the tip of a sharp knife, arrange all chicken pieces on a heated platter with the corn fritters. Keep warm.

To garnish: fry or broil the bacon slices until crisp, drain and arrange around the chicken. Serve the sauce separately.

Fold the beaten egg whites into the corn mixture

To Prepare Corn Kernels

Special corn scrapers are available which detach the kernels from the cob without losing the milk. Otherwise, cut kernels neatly from cob with a sharp knife.

To extract corn pulp when serving corn cream-style, slit through the center of each row of kernels with a sharp knife. Push out pulp and the milk with the back of knife.

Note: be careful when making corn fritters as they may pop when put in hot fat.

Accompaniment to Entrée

Green Salad with Fresh Pineapple

Boston, or Bibb, lettuce
1 small fresh pineapple
1 tablespoon sugar

For vinaigrette dressing
2 tablespoons wine vinegar
6 tablespoons oil
salt
black pepper, freshly ground
1 teaspoon chopped parsley
  (optional)

Method

Cut skin and plume from the pineapple, thinly slice the flesh and cut away the core. Sprinkle slices with sugar and refrigerate for at least 30 minutes. Wash lettuce, drain and wrap in a clean dish towel or paper towels. Chill until crisp.

To prepare the vinaigrette dressing: add seasonings to vinegar and gradually beat in oil with a fork or whisk until mixture emulsifies (oil is absorbed by the vinegar and there is no separation). Taste and adjust seasoning and pour a little dressing over the pineapple.

Just before serving, arrange in salad bowl; toss with enough dressing to coat each leaf. Add pineapple to lettuce, sprinkle with chopped parsley and serve at once.

Fried or broiled chicken is garnished with slices of crisp bacon

Caramel and vanilla bavarois is topped with rosettes of whipped cream and decorated with crushed caramel

Dessert

Caramel and Vanilla Bavarois

For caramel custard mixture
$\frac{1}{2}$ cup water
$\frac{1}{2}$ cup sugar
$1\frac{1}{4}$ cups milk
3 egg yolks
2 tablespoons sugar
1 tablespoon gelatin
5 tablespoons water
$\frac{1}{4}$ cup heavy cream

For vanilla custard mixture
$1\frac{1}{4}$ cups milk
1 vanilla bean, or $\frac{1}{2}$ teaspoon
   vanilla extract
3 egg yolks
3 tablespoons sugar
1 tablespoon gelatin
5 tablespoons water
$\frac{1}{4}$ cup heavy cream

For sauce and decoration
$\frac{1}{3}$ cup sugar
$\frac{3}{4}$ cup water
$\frac{1}{2}$ cup heavy cream

8 inch angel cake pan; cake pan for caramel decoration; pastry bag and medium star tube

An angel cake pan with its hollow center is particularly effective for this dessert, but a deep, round mold can certainly be used. Serves 6 people.

Method
To make caramel-flavored custard: put $\frac{1}{4}$ cup water in a saucepan, dissolve $\frac{1}{2}$ cup sugar in it and boil mixture until it is a rich brown caramel color. Pour remaining $\frac{1}{4}$ cup water into hot caramel and stir until caramel is dissolved. Stir in the milk.
Watchpoint: for protection when adding water to hot caramel, cover the hand holding pan with a dish towel or glove. The mixture will sizzle furiously.
   Cream egg yolks and 2 tablespoons sugar together until light. Stir in caramel milk, return to saucepan and cook the custard over a low heat, stirring constantly, until thick enough to coat the back of a wooden spoon.
Watchpoint: after adding the eggs, the mixture should never boil or it will curdle.
   Strain the custard and let cool.
   To make vanilla custard: put milk in a pan with vanilla bean (if using vanilla extract, add to custard after cooking). Heat almost to a boil; let stand 10 minutes to infuse. Cream egg yolks with sugar until light, stir in milk (after removing vanilla bean) and cook over a low heat, stirring constantly, until custard is thick enough to coat the spoon. Do not let it boil. Strain and cool. (If using vanilla extract, stir in at this point.)
   In a small pan soak gelatin for caramel custard in the 5 tablespoons water for 5 minutes or until spongy. In a separate pan soak gelatin for vanilla custard also in 5 tablespoons water. Dissolve both batches separately over a pan of hot water. Add one batch to the vanilla custard; the second batch to the caramel custard. Set pan containing caramel custard in a bowl filled with cold water and ice cubes and stir occasionally until it begins to set.
Watchpoint: it is important to stir the mixture occasionally or the custard will not set smoothly.
   Stiffly whip $\frac{1}{4}$ cup cream and fold into the caramel custard; pour mixture into the lightly oiled pan.
   Cool vanilla custard in the same way as the caramel custard, and as the custard begins to set, stiffly whip $\frac{1}{4}$ cup cream and fold in.
   Pour vanilla custard into cake pan and swirl a knife through the two mixtures to give a marbled effect. (Cake pan will not be filled to the top.) Chill until firm.
   To prepare sauce: in a saucepan dissolve sugar in half the water and boil until it is a rich brown caramel color. Pour a little onto the lightly oiled cake pan and let set until firm. This is the caramel decoration. Slowly add remaining water to caramel in saucepan (remember to cover the hand holding the pan with a towel or glove). Stir until all the caramel is dissolved. Pour sauce into a bowl and let cool.
   Loosen the sides of the bavarois with a table knife or spatula, easing it down to bottom at one spot and letting in a little air to release the vacuum. Put serving dish over the top of the pan and invert. Hold plate and pan and shake once or twice from side to side. At this point the bavarois should slip out easily.
Watchpoint: never dip a creamy dessert such as a bavarois into hot water to loosen it from the mold. This spoils the appearance. Only with aspic and fruit gelatin dishes is hot water used to release the molds.
   To decorate: whip remaining $\frac{1}{2}$ cup heavy cream until firm enough to pipe. Crush the sheet of caramel in the cake pan into small pieces. Pipe rosettes of whipped cream on top of bavarois and decorate with crushed caramel. Serve sauce separately.

Very carefully add water to the pan of hot caramel — it sizzles furiously, so protect the hand holding the pan with a dish towel or glove

Bavarian cream (bavarois) is a rich egg custard stiffened or set with gelatin, with whipped cream added.

How to COOK FISH

Fish on ice here are (clockwise): red snapper, rainbow trout, spots, Spanish mackerel and sea bass on the rack in the poacher

Fish is one of the most delicate foods and must be treated carefully. Too often it is not absolutely fresh or is overcooked. If it flakes easily when tested with a fork or if it is opaque right through the middle, the fish is done.

One of the best ways to cook fish is to poach it, whole or in steaks, and serve it with a good contrasting sauce. To poach means to cook in a small quantity of liquid in the oven or on top of the stove.

Poaching should be done in a special stock called a court bouillon rather than in water. This stock is simple to prepare, and once the fish has been cooked in it, the strained liquid can be used again for poaching or to make a sauce to serve with the fish. All poached fish should be thoroughly drained and transferred to a clean serving dish before being covered with sauce.

Cooking fish 'au gratin' is less well known. Small whole fish, fillets or steaks are cooked in the oven in a thick, well-seasoned sauce and finished with a topping of browned crumbs, melted butter and sometimes with cheese.

Fish can be divided into two main groups — rich fish, in which the fat is distributed throughout the body, and white fish, where the fat is contained in the liver.

Rich fish, like salmon, mackerel, herring, eel and shad, is usually cooked simply by broiling or poaching, or by sautéing in a little butter.

Flounder, cod, haddock, whitefish and perch are the most common white fish, but there are at least a dozen others available in different parts of the country. They are often deep-fried, poached, sautéed, or broiled, and are enhanced by a rich sauce.

Fish deteriorates more quickly than meat or poultry so refrigeration and rapid handling are very important. Fresh fish has little or no odor, bright eyes, red gills and a shiny skin.

Advice on frying fish was given in Volume 1 and a broiling lesson will be included in Volume 3.

Poaching Fish

A large poached fish, served cold and decorated with cucumber, tomato and watercress, then glazed with aspic or coated with mayonnaise, makes a spectacular centerpiece for a buffet. Salmon is the favorite choice for this dish, but sea or striped bass is a good and more economical alternative.

Hot fish, poached whole, should be well drained and served on a folded white napkin on a platter — the napkin absorbs any moisture. Hollandaise sauce, served separately, is the usual accompaniment.

Poach large cuts or steaks of fish and serve in the same way — the center cut is generally regarded as the best piece.

Allow $\frac{1}{2}$–$\frac{3}{4}$ lb fish per person, depending on the amount of bone and whether the head is included. The fish should be cleaned and trimmed of gills and fins but the scales can be left on a salmon or other fish with small scales. These give protection and make the fish easier to skin when cooked. Traditionally whole poached fish are served with the head on, but a whole fish, with head, can be hard to find unless specifically ordered.

Wash the fish, dry it thoroughly with paper towels and trim the tail to a 'vandyke' (i.e. follow the line of the tail and trim the center to a sharp 'V'). Leave on the head.

For a large fish, a fish poacher with a lift-out draining rack is very helpful as the fish must be covered completely with liquid to poach it properly. The rack enables you to remove the fish without it breaking. If a fish poacher is not available, wrap the fish in cheesecloth, leaving a length of cloth at each end so the fish can be lifted out easily, and cook it in a deep roasting pan.

A whole fish can be cooked in salted water, but the flavor is improved if court bouillon is used. For pieces or steaks of fish, it is essential to use court bouillon. Add the liquid when tepid for whole fish and large pieces, and when hot for steaks (this prevents too much seepage from the fish). Timing starts when the liquid is added.

If steaks are to be eaten cold, the flavor is improved even more by adding $\frac{1}{4}$ cup wine to court bouillon.

Cooking Times

Whole fish (over 5 lb): 6 minutes per lb
Whole fish or middle cuts (under 5 lb): 8 minutes per lb
Whole fish (under 2 lb): 10–20 minutes per fish
Steaks: 10–12 minutes, according to thickness.

Smaller fish can be cooked in a moderate oven (350°F) in an ovenproof dish with a small amount of liquid if basted often, or you can wrap it in foil.

When cooked, the fish should flake easily when tested with a fork. Carefully lift from fish kettle and drain a few minutes on paper towels. Remove the skin and the small bones along the center back. Transfer to a platter and serve hot. If fish is to be served cold, chill and decorate.

If steaks are to be served cold, let them cool in the cooking liquid before removing from the fish kettle, then drain and transfer to a serving platter.

Steaming Fish

For a thick steak or large piece of fish, first season and then wrap in buttered foil. Cook in a steamer or fish kettle, allowing 20 minutes per lb. If serving cold, cool the fish before unwrapping.

Note: for detailed instructions on preparing fish, see pages 118–119.

Court Bouillon

For 4 cup quantity, combine 4 cups water, 1 sliced carrot, 1 small onion (sliced and stuck with a clove), bouquet garni, 6 peppercorns and 2 tablespoons vinegar, or lemon juice, in a pan with a little salt. Cover, bring to a boil and simmer 15–20 minutes. Strain and use.

RICH FISH

Salmon

The rich flavor and succulent flesh of salmon make it the king of table fish. As a result, it has been greatly overfished and is now non-existent in East Coast rivers. The commercial supply comes from the Pacific Coast and Canada.

Salmon is basically a salt-water fish which returns to rivers only to spawn in spring. This is where it is caught and the season for the best fresh Chinook salmon lasts from late spring through July, although frozen salmon is available in many fish markets all year. A large salmon can weigh up to 60 lb, but the usual size in retail markets is 12–16 lb.

To develop its full flavor, salmon is best poached in court bouillon and served hot with Hollandaise sauce or cold with a herb, tomato or plain homemade mayonnaise. It can also be wrapped in foil with herbs and butter and baked in a moderate oven or, if cut in steaks, sautéed in butter and served with Hollandaise or Béarnaise sauce.

Salmon Steaks with Madeira Sauce

4 salmon steaks, 1 inch thick
$\frac{1}{4}$ cup seasoned flour (made with $\frac{1}{4}$ teaspoon salt and pinch of pepper)
$\frac{1}{4}$ cup butter
$1\frac{1}{2}$ cups ($\frac{1}{3}$ lb) small mushrooms

For Madeira sauce
$\frac{1}{4}$ cup Madeira
1 cup heavy cream
kneaded butter (made with 2 tablespoons butter and 1 tablespoon flour)
salt and pepper

Method

Dry steaks well with paper towels and coat them with seasoned flour. In a skillet heat 2 tablespoons of the butter; sauté steaks for 3–4 minutes over medium heat or until brown. Turn over, brown on the other side, arrange on a platter and keep warm.

Melt remaining butter in the skillet and add the mushrooms, with the stems trimmed level with the caps. Sauté until tender, turning once, and pile a few on top of each steak.

Deglaze the pan with the Madeira, and simmer until liquid is reduced to 2 tablespoons. Stir in cream, bring almost to a boil and strain into a saucepan. Reheat and add the kneaded butter in small pieces, stirring constantly, until the sauce is the consistency of thin cream. Simmer 2 minutes, season to taste and spoon over the steaks.

Baked Stuffed Salmon

2 lb center cut of salmon
$\frac{1}{4}$ cup butter
salt and pepper

For stuffing
2 tablespoons butter
1 onion, finely chopped
$\frac{1}{2}$ cup finely chopped, or ground cooked ham
1 cup fresh white breadcrumbs
2 tablespoons chopped parsley
1 teaspoon tarragon
1 egg
milk (to moisten)
salt and pepper

Method

For stuffing: melt butter in a pan and sauté onion until soft but not browned. Add to the ham, breadcrumbs, parsley and tarragon in a bowl and stir in egg with enough milk to make a soft stuffing. Season to taste.

Wash and dry salmon, fill cavity with stuffing and place fish on a sheet of foil. Spread the $\frac{1}{4}$ cup butter over the fish, sprinkle with salt and pepper and wrap securely. Place in a baking dish and bake in a moderate oven (350°F) for 30 minutes or until fish flakes easily when tested with a fork. Unwrap foil, place fish on a platter, pour over any juices and serve.

Serve a sharp mustard sauce with baked, stuffed herring Calaisienne

Herring

Herring are a little smaller than mackerel and also taste best when eaten very fresh.

Herring are well known in many forms. Pickled and salted herring are available in supermarkets; kippered and smoked herring, which are carried by most fish markets, make excellent pâté.

Fresh herring are mistakenly neglected, for they are a succulent fish with plenty of flavor. They can be broiled, or are delicious cooked as in Scotland — rolled in oatmeal and fried in lard or bacon fat.

Soused Herring

6 herring, split, with backbone removed
salt and pepper
1 tablespoon pickling spice
1 onion, thinly sliced
1 cup wine vinegar, or white wine
1 cup water

Method
Season cut surface of herring with salt and pepper and roll up from head to tail. Pack in a deep baking dish or casserole. Combine pickling spice, onion, vinegar and water in a pan with a pinch of salt and bring to a boil. Pour over the herring — the liquid should just cover them. Bake in a moderately low oven (325°F) for 1 hour. Serve cold.

Herring Calaisienne with Mustard Sauce

4 herring (with soft roes), split, with backbones removed
2 tablespoons butter
1 tablespoon finely chopped onion
1 teaspoon chopped parsley
1 teaspoon thyme
2 eggs, hard-cooked and chopped
1 clove of garlic, crushed
pepper
2 slices of bread, soaked in a little milk
grated rind of $\frac{1}{2}$ lemon
1 cup mustard sauce (see page 46 or 53)

Method

Wash herring and dry well.

In a small pan, melt 1 tablespoon of the butter, add onion and cook slowly until soft but not browned. Chop soft roes and combine in a bowl with herbs, hard-cooked eggs, garlic and pepper. Squeeze the liquid from the bread, chop and add to the mixture with the lemon rind and cooked onion. Mix well to bind.

Stuff the mixture into the herring, reshape and place in a buttered ovenproof dish. Spread with remaining butter, cover with buttered foil and bake in a moderately hot oven (350°F) for 25 minutes, or until fish flakes easily when tested with a fork.

Pour the mustard sauce into a deep platter and arrange the herring on top. Serve hot.

Pickling spice is a mixture of whole spices (peppercorns, allspice, mace, etc.) and is a convenient way of buying spices if you do not often use them. If not using pickling spice for soused herring, you will need 6 peppercorns, 2 blades of mace, 2 allspice berries, 1 bay leaf and 1 clove. For a milder flavored souse, add 1 tablespoon brown sugar to vinegar (or white wine) and water.

Eel

Eel migrate like salmon from saltwater to freshwater and are caught in either. They are rarely sold fresh except in Italian markets, but smoked eel makes a delicious and unusual appetizer. 'Spitchcock' eel are split down the back ready for broiling.

Shad

Shad is one of the gastronomic pleasures of late winter and spring. Like salmon, it has so much flavor of its own that it is best treated simply.

Whole shad, which average 4–5 lb, are frequently stuffed and baked. However, shad fillets are the most popular, as the fish is full of small bones which only an expert knows how to extract. The fillets are most often broiled or sautéed in butter, but they are also excellent baked in cream.

Shad roe is a delicacy that is a good deal more expensive than the fish itself. Usually the roe is fried or broiled and served with bacon, or it can be cooked and served with fillets of the fish.

Shad Roe with Bacon

2 pairs of shad roe
$\frac{1}{2}$ cup butter
1 tablespoon chopped parsley
salt and pepper
$\frac{1}{2}$ lb sliced bacon

Method

In a skillet melt butter, add roe and sauté over low heat for about 15 minutes or until the roe are tender, turning once. Arrange on a platter and sprinkle with parsley and seasoning. Fry bacon until crisp and lay on top of the roe.

Baked Shad with Lemon Stuffing

4 large shad, or 8 small shad fillets
2 tablespoons butter
$1\frac{1}{2}$ cups light cream
salt and pepper

For stuffing
$\frac{1}{4}$ cup butter
2 onions, chopped
1 cup fresh white breadcrumbs
3 tablespoons chopped parsley
grated rind of 2 lemons
1 egg
2 tablespoons lemon juice

Method

To make stuffing: in a skillet melt butter, add onions and sauté until soft but not browned. Add to the breadcrumbs, parsley and lemon rind in a bowl. Stir in egg and lemon juice and season to taste.

Wash and dry fish or fillets. Fill cavity of whole fish with stuffing or spread it on half the fillets and lay the remaining ones on top. Place fish in a buttered baking dish, dot with butter, pour over the cream and sprinkle with salt and pepper. Cover dish with foil and bake in a moderately hot oven (375°F) for 45–55 minutes for the whole fish, or 25–30 minutes for the fillets, or until fish flakes easily when tested with a fork. Transfer to a platter and serve.

'Fish' Potatoes

These are shaped from large white potatoes and are so named because they frequently accompany fish dishes.

Choose medium-sized potatoes, peel and quarter them lengthwise. Pare away the sharp edges with a peeler and shape them into ovals. Boil in a pan of salted water for about 7 minutes, drain and return them to the pan.

Cover with foil and the pan lid and continue cooking 4–5 minutes over a very low heat or until tender.

This method prevents the potatoes from breaking and makes them dry and floury.

Fried mackerel fillets are garnished with mushrooms and onion mixture and sautéed tomato slices

Mackerel

Mackerel are a rich, firm fish with a definite flavor. They must be eaten as fresh as possible as they quickly become oily and unpalatable if kept too long.

Good mackerel run up to 16 inches long and are easiest to cope with if filleted before cooking. Thoroughly dry the fillets, roll them in seasoned flour or cornmeal and fry in bacon fat or butter; alternatively, they may be broiled. Serve sizzling hot with quarters of lemon.

If this is too rich for your tastes, try poaching the fillets in a moderately hot oven (375°F) for 10–15 minutes in a little salted water with the juice of $\frac{1}{2}$ lemon. Drain and serve with a sprinkling of chopped parsley and boiled or 'fish' potatoes (see page 109).

Mackerel with Mushrooms and Tomatoes

2–3 mackerel (according to size), filleted
$\frac{1}{2}$ cup seasoned flour (made with $\frac{1}{2}$ teaspoon salt and $\frac{1}{4}$ teaspoon pepper
$\frac{1}{4}$ cup oil
1 small onion, finely chopped
1 cup finely chopped mushrooms
1 clove of garlic, chopped
2 teaspoons chopped mixed herbs (basil, tarragon, dill, parsley)
2 tablespoons wine vinegar
salt and pepper
3 tomatoes, skinned and sliced

Method
Prepare the mackerel fillets, if necessary. Wash and dry them and roll in seasoned flour. In a frying pan or skillet heat 2 tablespoons of the oil. When very hot, put in the fillets, cut side down, and fry over medium heat for 3 minutes or until brown; turn and brown on the other side.

Lift out fillets and arrange them, overlapping, on a platter; keep warm in a low oven.

Wipe out the pan, reheat and add 1 more tablespoon of oil. Add onion and cook gently until soft but not browned. Add mushrooms and garlic and cook briskly for 2–3 minutes until all moisture has evaporated. Stir in herbs and vinegar and season to taste. Bring to a boil and spoon over the fish.

Sauté tomatoes in remaining oil over very high heat for 1–2 minutes or until lightly cooked. Do not allow them to become mushy. Sprinkle with salt and pepper, arrange around the fish or at each end of the platter and serve.

Mackerel with Venetian Sauce

2–3 mackerel (according to size), filleted
salt
squeeze of lemon juice

For Venetian sauce
1 small cucumber, peeled, seeded and diced
$\frac{1}{4}$ package (2–3 oz) fresh spinach leaves
sprig of tarragon, or $\frac{1}{2}$ teaspoon dried tarragon
sprig of chervil, or $\frac{1}{2}$ teaspoon dried chervil
5 tablespoons butter
2 teaspoons flour
1 cup water
salt and pepper
2 egg yolks
2 shallots, or scallions, finely chopped

Method
Fillet the fish if this has not already been done. Wash and dry fillets, lay them in a baking dish and barely cover with water. Add salt and a good squeeze of lemon juice, cover with foil and poach in a moderate oven (350°F) for 12–15 minutes, or until the fish flakes easily when tested with a fork.

To make Venetian sauce: blanch cucumber for 3 minutes in boiling salted water, drain and set aside. Cook spinach and herbs in boiling salted water for 5 minutes. Drain them, squeeze in a piece of cheesecloth or the end of a clean dish towel to remove moisture, and rub through a wire strainer or purée in a blender.

In a pan melt 1 tablespoon of the butter and stir in flour. Whisk in the water with a little salt and pepper, bring just to a boil and take from heat. Beat in egg yolks and remaining butter, a small piece at a time. Add spinach and herb purée and taste for seasoning.

Take out fish, drain and arrange on a platter. Pour liquid into a pan, add shallots or scallions and boil until reduced to 3–4 tablespoons. Strain into the sauce. Reheat sauce gently without boiling, add cucumber and spoon down center of fish. Serve hot.

Mackerel à la Provençale

4 mackerel, cleaned and trimmed
$\frac{1}{4}$ cup olive oil
2 medium onions, chopped
4 tomatoes, peeled, seeded and chopped
2 cloves of garlic, crushed
3 green peppers, or 2 green and 1 red, cored, seeded and cut in strips
1 teaspoon basil
1 tablespoon chopped parsley
3 tablespoons tomato purée
salt and pepper

In Provence, France, this dish is made with fresh sardines, similar in texture to mackerel.

Method
Heat oil and sauté onion until soft but not browned. Add tomatoes and garlic and cook 2 minutes, stirring occasionally. Add peppers, basil, parsley and tomato purée with seasoning to taste and cook 2 minutes longer. Lay mackerel in an oiled baking dish, and spoon tomato mixture over the top. Cover tightly with a lid or foil and bake in a hot oven (400°F) for 30 minutes or until mackerel flakes easily when tested with a fork.

Serve hot, garnished with chopped parsley, or cold, decorated with thin slices of lemon, chopped capers and parsley.

WHITE FISH

Cod

An average cod weighs about 10 lb, but fish as large as 60 lb have been caught in the fishing waters off Newfoundland. Small cod, of $1\frac{1}{2}$–2 lb are called scrod.

To serve this creamy fish at its best, wash and dry it, then rub the surface with a freshly cut lemon and lightly sprinkle it with salt. Cover and leave for $\frac{1}{2}$–1 hour in the refrigerator. Before using, drain off any liquid and dry the fish again.

Cod has a robust flavor which stands up well on its own or combines splendidly with other distinctive ingredients. Try poaching it like salmon and serving it hot with an egg sauce, based on béchamel, or an oyster, shrimp or lobster sauce made by adding cooked shellfish to a béchamel sauce. Genevoise or Venetian sauces are also good with cod.

Cod Steaks Bretonne

4 large cod steaks, 1 inch thick
squeeze of lemon juice
salt and pepper
$\frac{1}{4}$ cup water
$\frac{3}{4}$ cup apple cider
2 tablespoons butter
1 medium carrot, cut in julienne strips
1 medium onion, cut in julienne strips
2 stalks of celery, cut in julienne strips
1 tablespoon flour
3 tablespoons light cream
2 teaspoons chopped parsley

Method
Wash fish and dry with paper towels. Sprinkle lightly with lemon juice and salt. Let stand $\frac{1}{2}$–1 hour in the refrigerator, drain off any liquid and dry fish again.

Place steaks in buttered ovenproof dish, pour over the water with half the cider, cover with buttered paper and poach in a moderate oven (350°F) for 10–15 minutes, or until fish flakes easily.

In a saucepan melt $\frac{1}{2}$ tablespoon of the butter, add carrot, onion and celery, 1 tablespoon of remaining cider and salt and pepper. Cover tightly, cook 2–3 minutes on top of stove, then put in moderate oven (350°F) and continue cooking 15 minutes or until vegetables are tender.

Drain fish, reserving the liquid, and carefully remove center bone and outer skin, leaving the steak unbroken. Arrange on a hot platter and spoon the vegetables on top. Keep warm.

Strain reserved liquid into a saucepan, add remaining cider and boil 2–3 minutes to reduce. Make kneaded butter, using flour and remaining butter and add to liquid in 2–3 pieces, off the heat. Bring to a boil, stirring constantly, and simmer 2–3 minutes. Add cream and parsley and taste for seasoning. The sauce should be the consistency of thin cream. If necessary, add more kneaded butter.

Spoon sauce over fish and vegetables and serve.

Cod Kebabs

$1\frac{1}{2}$–2 lb cod, in the piece or cut in thick steaks
salt and pepper
juice of $\frac{1}{2}$ lemon
1 large onion
16 small mushrooms
8–12 bay leaves
1 teaspoon thyme
$\frac{1}{2}$ cup butter

4 large kebab skewers

Method
Cut cod into 1 inch cubes, removing bones and skin. Sprinkle with salt and lemon juice, cover and stand 30 minutes. Drain off any liquid and dry on paper towels.

Peel and quarter the onion and separate the layers. Trim mushroom stems level with caps. Spear cod, onion and mushrooms on the skewers, adding two or three pieces of bay leaf per skewer. Sprinkle with salt, pepper and thyme.

Melt the butter in a skillet and sauté kebabs over medium heat until browned on all sides or broil them, basting often with melted butter.

Broiled Cod with Paprika

$1\frac{1}{2}$–2 lb cod fillets or steaks, cut 1 inch thick
2 teaspoons paprika
$\frac{1}{2}$ cup butter
1 onion, very finely chopped
$\frac{1}{4}$ teaspoon cayenne
$\frac{1}{2}$ teaspoon salt
1 tablespoon lemon juice
1 tablespoon chopped parsley (for garnish)

Method
Heat the broiler.

In a pan melt 2 tablespoons of the butter and sauté the onion until soft. Add the paprika and cayenne and cook gently for 2 minutes longer, stirring occasionally. Add the salt, lemon juice and remaining butter and heat until melted.

Set the fish on a broiler rack and brush with the paprika mixture. Broil about 2 inches from the heat for 4–5 minutes, brushing with more of the paprika mixture once or twice. Turn, brush with the remaining butter and broil 4–5 minutes longer or until the fish is browned and flakes easily. Transfer to a platter, sprinkle with parsley and serve with caramelized tomatoes (see page 84).

Broiled Cod with Herbs and Garlic

Cod is one of the few fish with a flavor that is robust enough to go with garlic.

Follow recipe for broiled cod with paprika, but omit paprika and cayenne. Instead add 1–2 cloves of garlic, crushed, 2 teaspoons chopped chives and 1 teaspoon dill to butter mixture with lemon juice. Continue as above.

Cod steaks Bretonne, poached in cider, are finished in a cream sauce

Salt Cod à l'Espagnole

1½ lb salt cod

For sauce
4 tablespoons olive oil
2 medium onions, chopped
2 cloves of garlic, crushed
2 green peppers, cored,
   seeded and cut in strips
6 tomatoes, peeled, seeded
   and chopped
salt and pepper

Method

Soak cod in cold water for 4 hours or according to package directions.

To make the sauce: in a skillet heat oil and fry onions until soft but not browned. Add garlic, peppers and tomatoes with salt and pepper to taste and simmer over low heat, stirring occasionally, for 20 minutes or until the sauce is thick.

Rinse cod thoroughly, put in a shallow flameproof dish, cover with cold water and bring to a boil. Cover and simmer gently for 15 minutes, or until cod flakes easily. Drain well, add to the sauce and keep over very low heat for 10 minutes so the flavors can blend.

Transfer to a platter and serve with boiled rice.

> In France it used to be the practice to cook **salt cod** in rainwater and always in an earthenware casserole. This is still sometimes done today and the pure water enhances the fish's flavor.

Morue Louasardaise (Salt Cod Louasardaise)

1½ lb salt cod
½ cup milk
½ cup water
4 medium potatoes, peeled
3 tablespoons butter
⅓ cup hot milk
salt and pepper
½ lb cooked, peeled shrimps
6 hard-cooked eggs, chopped
2 tablespoons grated
   Parmesan cheese
béchamel sauce, made with
   5 tablespoons butter,
   5 tablespoons flour and
   3 cups milk (infused with
   slice of onion, 6 peppercorns, blade of mace and
   bay leaf)
2 tablespoons heavy cream

This recipe can also be made with fresh cod or finnan haddie, and the cooking time should be reduced to 15–20 minutes.

Method

Soak the salt cod for 8–12 hours in several changes of cold water. Wash and dry the cod, place in a baking dish, pour over the milk and water and cover with buttered foil. Bake in moderate oven (350°F) for 30 minutes or until the fish flakes easily. Drain well and flake fish, discarding the skin and bones.

Cook the potatoes in boiling salted water for 15–20 minutes or until tender and drain. Mash them and beat in the butter and enough hot milk to make a smooth purée; season well.

Make the béchamel sauce and keep warm.

In a soufflé dish or baking dish, layer the sauce with the flaked fish, shrimps and chopped eggs, beginning and ending with a layer of sauce. Spread the potato purée on top and sprinkle with Parmesan cheese. Bake in a hot oven (400°F) for 10–15 minutes or until browned.

Watchpoint: do not let the dish become too hot or the sauce will curdle.

Haddock

This large round fish looks like cod although it is smaller and generally weighs up to 6 lb. It is distinguishable by the dark line down each side and a black 'finger' mark behind each gill, known as St. Peter's mark. Haddock is generally sold in fillets and it is often smoked to make finnan haddie, named after the fishing port of Findon in Scotland.

Finnan Haddie Cakes

1 lb finnan haddie fillet
1½ cups milk
1½ cups mashed potatoes
¼ teaspoon ground mace
salt and pepper
1 egg, beaten to mix
½ cup seasoned flour (made
   with ½ teaspoon salt and
   ¼ teaspoon pepper)
¼ cup butter

Method

Pour milk over finnan haddie, cover with buttered foil and bake in a moderate oven (350°F) for 20 minutes, or until the fish flakes easily. Drain and flake fish, removing any bones and skin.

Combine finnan haddie, potatoes, and mace with seasoning to taste. Stir in egg and shape mixture into small round cakes about ¾ inch thick. Coat in seasoned flour. Heat butter in a skillet, add cakes and fry over medium heat until golden on both sides. Serve with ravigote or caper sauce (see pages 46 or 53).

Haddock with Paprika and Mushrooms

1½–2 lb haddock fillet
½ cup water
juice of ½ lemon
salt

For sauce
1 cup (¼ lb) sliced mushrooms
5 tablespoons butter
1 tablespoon paprika
black pepper, freshly ground
3 tablespoons flour
2 cups milk
2 slices of canned pimiento,
   drained and cut in strips

Method

Cut fish into portions, or tuck under the ends of small fillets, and lay in a buttered ovenproof dish, skinned side down. Pour over water and lemon juice and sprinkle with a little salt, cover with buttered foil and poach in a moderate oven (350°F) for 15 minutes, or until the fish flakes easily.

To make sauce: in a saucepan melt half the butter and sauté mushrooms 2 minutes or until soft. Take from heat, add paprika and remaining butter with a little seasoning. Heat to melt the butter, stir in flour off heat and add milk. Bring to a boil, stirring, and set aside.

Drain fish and transfer to a platter. Strain poaching liquid into sauce, bring to a boil, and simmer to reduce for 1–2 minutes. Add pimiento strips and spoon sauce over fish. Serve with noodles tossed in melted butter.

Haddock au Gratin

1½–2 lb haddock fillet
salt and pepper
1 cup (¼ lb) mushrooms,
    sliced and cooked in a little
    butter (optional)
¼ cup grated cheese
browned breadcrumbs

For sauce
3 tablespoons butter
3 tablespoons flour
1½ cups milk

Method
Cut fish into portions if the fillets are large and lay them in a buttered ovenproof dish. If using whole fillets, tuck each end under before placing them in the dish. The side nearest the bones should be uppermost as this is always the whitest. Season lightly.

To make sauce: melt butter in a saucepan and stir in flour off heat. Pour on milk, return to heat and bring to a boil, stirring continuously. Simmer 2–3 minutes, season and spoon over the fish, coating it completely. Sprinkle with grated cheese and breadcrumbs and bake in a moderate oven (350°F) for 20–25 minutes, or until fish flakes easily.

Sliced cooked mushrooms can be spooned over the fish before it is coated with this sauce, or a mushroom sauce can be used (see page 45).

Watchpoint: the sauce for fish cooked in this way should be thicker than ordinary coating sauce to allow for dilution by the juices from the fish. This is why the pieces of fish should be laid flat and completely cover the base of the dish; otherwise the liquid will not blend properly with the sauce and might leave a watery liquid at the edge of the dish.

Baked Haddock Nicoise

4 haddock steaks, cut 1 inch
    thick
¼ cup oil
2 onions, sliced
3 tomatoes, peeled, seeded
    and cut in strips, or 2 cups
    canned tomatoes, crushed
1 clove of garlic, crushed
¾ cup white wine
1 tablespoon chopped fresh
    fennel or 1 teaspoon fennel
    seeds, crushed
salt and pepper
1 tablespoon chopped parsley
3–4 strips of lemon rind

Method
In a flameproof casserole, heat half the oil and fry the onion until soft. Add the tomatoes with the garlic and cook 2 minutes. Set the haddock steaks on top, pour over the wine and sprinkle with chopped fennel or fennel seeds and seasoning.

Add the lemon rind and bake in a moderate oven (350°F) for 15 minutes or until the fish flakes easily. Sprinkle with parsley and serve with small boiled potatoes.

Haddock with Onions

1½–2 lb fillets of haddock
2–3 large onions, cut in rings
1½ cups water
squeeze of lemon juice
salt and pepper
2 tablespoons butter

For sauce
2 tablespoons butter
2 tablespoons flour
¾ cup light cream
1 teaspoon Dijon-style
    mustard
2 tablespoons grated dry
    Cheddar cheese

Method
Set oven at moderate (350°F).

Wash the fillets, dry and cut them in half if they are large. Lay them in a buttered baking dish, pour over the water, add a squeeze of lemon juice and seasoning. Cover with buttered foil and poach in heated oven for 10–12 minutes or until the fish flakes easily. Drain and keep warm; strain liquid and reserve.

Melt the 2 tablespoons butter in a shallow saucepan, add the onion rings with a little seasoning.

Watchpoint: if the onions seem strongly flavored, blanch in boiling water for 1 minute before cooking in the butter.

Press a piece of buttered foil on top of the onions and cover tightly with the lid. Cook very slowly for 10–12 minutes or until soft but not browned. Transfer to flameproof platter and keep warm.

To make the sauce: melt the butter in a saucepan, stir in the flour off the heat and pour in the reserved cooking liquid. Bring to a boil and simmer 5 minutes or until the sauce is reduced by about one-quarter. Add the cream, bring back to a boil, season; simmer 2–3 minutes longer.

Arrange the fillets on top of the onions, stir the mustard and half the cheese into the sauce, adjust the seasoning and spoon sauce over fish. Sprinkle remaining cheese on top and brown under broiler.

Ocean Perch or Redfish

Any frozen package labeled white fish fillets is likely to be ocean perch because it is the most common fish on the market. The flesh is firm and slightly coarse and the flavor bland, so it is best combined with well-flavored ingredients.

Perch Diable

1½–2 lb perch fillets
2 cups court bouillon
    (see page 107)

For sauce
1 cup heavy cream
1 teaspoon anchovy paste
2 teaspoons Worcestershire
    sauce
salt, pepper, dry mustard
pinch of cayenne
2 teaspoons mango chutney

Method
Lay fillets in a buttered ovenproof dish, tucking the ends under, and pour over the court bouillon. Cover with buttered foil and bake in a moderate oven (350°F) 12–15 minutes until fish flakes easily. Drain; arrange in ovenproof dish.

To make sauce: stiffly whip cream, gradually add remaining ingredients, except the chutney, whisking gently to keep the sauce as thick as possible. Season to taste, fold in chutney and spoon sauce over fish. Bake in a very hot oven (450°F) for 5 minutes and serve at once.

Baked haddock niçoise is garnished with chopped parsley (recipe is on page 115)

Perch Alphonse XIII

1–1½ lb perch fillets
½ cup seasoned flour (made with ½ teaspoon salt and ¼ teaspoon pepper)
¼ cup butter

For garnish
2 small eggplants
¼ cup olive oil
1 tablespoon butter
1 onion, sliced
3 tomatoes, peeled, seeded and chopped, or 1 cup Italian-style canned tomatoes, crushed
1 clove of garlic, crushed with a little salt
1 teaspoon basil
salt and pepper
juice of ½ lemon
1 tablespoon chopped parsley

Method

To prepare garnish: halve eggplants lengthwise and slash the centers in a criss-cross pattern with a sharp knife. Sprinkle with salt, let stand 30 minutes and drain off any liquid. Brush cut surfaces with oil and bake in a moderate oven (350°F) for 25 minutes or until soft, brushing with oil from time to time. Scoop out flesh with a teaspoon and chop coarsely. Place eggplant skins in an ovenproof serving dish. Melt butter in a saucepan and cook onion until golden. Add tomatoes and garlic and simmer 15 minutes or until thick. Add basil, chopped eggplant flesh and seasoning. Spoon into eggplant skins and keep warm.

Melt half the butter in a skillet. Coat fillets in seasoned flour and place in skillet, skinned side up. Fry over moderate heat for 2–3 minutes until brown, turn and brown on the other side. Take out and arrange, overlapping, on eggplant skins. Wipe out pan, melt remaining butter and heat until it is a light brown. Immediately add lemon juice and parsley and pour over fish. Serve at once.

Perch Croquettes Vert Pré

1 lb perch, or any white fish, fillets
salt and pepper
6 peppercorns
squeeze of lemon juice
2 tablespoons water
2 medium potatoes
bunch of watercress
2 tablespoons butter
1 egg
fried parsley (for garnish)

For coating
¼ cup seasoned flour (made with pinch each of salt and pepper)
1 egg, beaten to mix
¾ cup dried white breadcrumbs
deep fat (for frying)

Method

Wash fish and place in a buttered ovenproof dish. Season with salt, add peppercorns, lemon juice and water, cover with buttered foil and bake in a moderate oven (350°F) for 10–12 minutes. Drain and flake with a fork, removing any bones.

Peel and quarter potatoes. Wash watercress and cook both together in a pan of boiling salted water until potatoes are just tender. Drain mixture well, dry in the pan for 5 minutes over very gentle heat, then push through a sieve or food mill.

Mix fish with potato and watercress purée, add butter, season to taste; add egg and beat well. Form mixture into cylindrical croquettes about 3 inches long and 1¼ inches in diameter, using a palette knife to flatten the ends. Roll croquettes in seasoned flour, coat with beaten egg and breadcrumbs. Fry in hot deep fat (360°F on a fat thermometer) for 3 minutes or until golden. Drain on paper towels. Serve croquettes, garnished with fried parsley, and a mustard or caper sauce separately (see pages 46 or 53).
Serve with fried onion rings.

> **Vert pré**, literally 'green meadow', usually refers to broiled meats topped with maître d'hôtel butter and garnished with watercress and very finely cut French fries called straw potatoes. Here, vert pré applies to croquettes, green from watercress and potato purée.

Cut onions into ¼ inch slices and separate them into rings

Fried Onion Rings

Peel 1–2 large Bermuda or Spanish onions, cut them into ¼ inch slices and separate them into rings. Barely cover them with milk, let soak 5 minutes, then drain.

Dip the rings first in 1 egg, beaten to mix, and then in seasoned flour. Fry them, a few at a time, in hot deep fat (375°F on a fat thermometer) until they are crisp and golden. Drain them thoroughly on crumpled paper towels and serve at once.

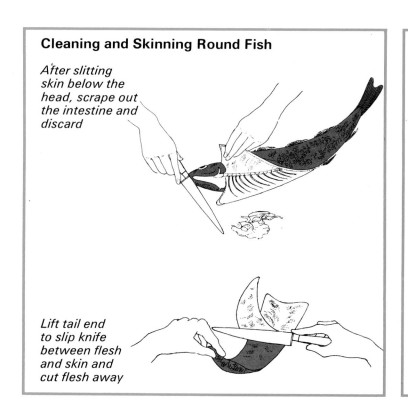

Cleaning and Skinning Round Fish

After slitting skin below the head, scrape out the intestine and discard

Lift tail end to slip knife between flesh and skin and cut flesh away

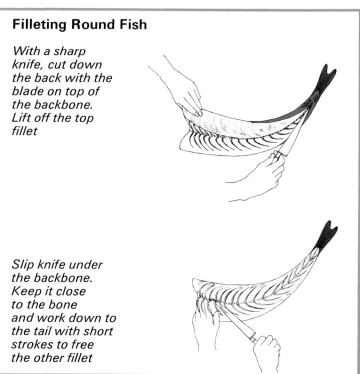

Filleting Round Fish

With a sharp knife, cut down the back with the blade on top of the backbone. Lift off the top fillet

Slip knife under the backbone. Keep it close to the bone and work down to the tail with short strokes to free the other fillet

How to prepare fresh fish

The fish sold in markets are already prepared or will be prepared to your order. Matters are different when you are faced with your first fresh catch. Here are instructions for cleaning, skinning and filleting round and flat fish.

To Clean Round Fish

Rinse in cold water; then, with a sharp, pointed knife, scrape with the back of the knife from tail to head to remove the scales. This applies particularly to scaly fish like red snapper.

For large round fish, such as haddock, take a sharp knife and slit the skin from below the head, along the belly to the vent. Scrape out intestines and discard. Leave head intact or cut it off, as you like. Hold the fish under cold running water to clean it thoroughly. If there is any black skin inside the cavity, gently rub it away with a damp cloth dipped in salt.

For small round fish which are to be left whole with the head on, like trout, hook a finger around the gills and pull them away (be careful as they may be quite sharp). Pull out the intestines through the hole left by the gills and rinse the cavity thoroughly. Trim the fins and tail with scissors.

To Skin Fillets of Round Fish

Lay the fish, skin side down, on a board, lift the tail end and slip a thin, sharp knife between the flesh and skin. Dip the fingers of your left hand in salt to prevent it from slipping and, holding the skin firmly, saw the flesh away from the skin, keeping the knife at an angle to the board.

To Fillet Round Fish

Lay the fish on a wet, rough cloth to prevent it from slipping and hold the fish steady with one hand. With a pair of scissors trim away the fins. Then cut down the back with a knife (there is a special knife for this called a filleting

Skinning Flat Fish

Cut off fins, slip thumb about 1 inch under the black skin at the cut where the fish was cleaned

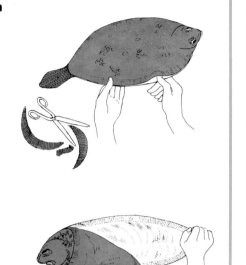

Run thumb around fish, keeping it under the skin. Grasp tail end firmly and rip off skin. Repeat on the other side

Filleting Flat Fish

Run knife down the backbone from the center of the head, out and down to the tail to lift off first half of the fillet

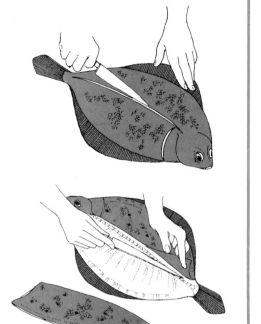

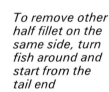

To remove other half fillet on the same side, turn fish around and start from the tail end

---

knife) on top of the backbone. Lift off the top fillet. Now slip the knife under the backbone at the head and, keeping it as close as possible to the backbone, work down to the tail, at the same time keeping a firm hold on the head with the other hand. Always cut with short sharp strokes of the knife.

To Clean Flat Fish
With fish like sole or flounder, make a semicircular cut just below the head on the dark side, scrape out the intestines and wash the fish thoroughly.

To Skin Flat Fish
Sole and flounder may be skinned when they are whole.

Trim away the outside fins with scissors. Lay the fish on a board and, starting at the head, slip your thumb about

1 inch under the black skin at the cut where the fish was cleaned. Run your thumb right around the fish, then grasp the tail end of the skin firmly and rip it off. Repeat this on the other side of the fish.

Flat fish with thick skins must be skinned like round fish after filleting as the skin will tear the flesh if you try to rip it off.

To Fillet Flat Fish
Flounder and sole (if weighing no more than 1½ lb) are usually cut by professionals into a double fillet so that the flesh on each side of the backbone is taken off in one piece, giving two fillets only for each fish. These may be divided in half for cooking.

At home it is easier to take the flesh off in four fillets. Run the point of the knife

down the backbone with short sharp strokes, keeping the knife in contact with the bone, work from the head out until the tail is reached and the fillet is detached. Turn the fish around and, starting from the tail, take off the other half

of the fillet in the same way. Turn the fish over and repeat the process. Flat fish fillets are larger and thicker on the dark side (that which is uppermost when the fish is swimming).

Short guide to French names of fish you're likely to find on a restaurant menu.

anchovy	anchois	mussel	moule
bass	bar	oyster	huître
carp	carpe	perch	perche
catfish	poisson-chat	pike	brochet
clam	palourde	salmon	saumon
cod	cabillaud	salt cod	morue
crab	crabe	scallop	coquille St. Jacques
crayfish	écrevisse	sea bass	loup de mer
eel	anguille	shad	alose
haddock	aiglefin	shrimp	crevette
halibut	flétan	smelt	éperlan
herring	hareng	swordfish	espadon
lobster	homard	trout	truite
mackerel	maquereau	tuna	thon

POTS AND PANS

Good cooks need good tools and none are more important than pots and pans. If you know from the beginning what to look for, your equipment need not be outrageously expensive.

Which metals are best? What design features are important? Is cleaning or heat conduction more vital? Which pans are essential; which are luxuries? These are just a few of the questions which confront you when on a serious pan shopping expedition.

If you keep in mind some basic facts about design, materials, and the essentials of a good kitchen, it will make your choice a great deal easier. Remember too, that design will affect cleaning and storage; materials will affect cooking time and control; and knowledge of essential pans will cut down on clutter and over-expenditure.

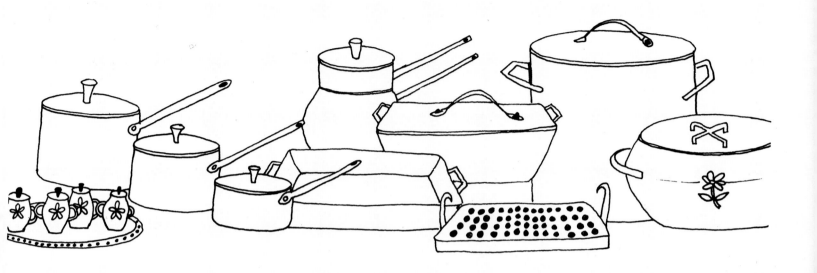

Design points to look for

Pan bottoms that are curved on the inside, smooth joints near the handle, and flowing lines throughout will make your pans easier to clean.

Flat lids will be most helpful for stacking if you don't plan to hang your pans on the wall. All lids and covers should fit snugly. Test knobs on lids; make sure they can be lifted easily and check that knobs are made of a non-heat-conducting material like wood or plastic.

Heavy pots and pans, or those with 5 pint or more capacity, should have more than one handle. When you're buying a pan, try lifting it to test which length and form of handle fits your hand most comfortably.

For limited budgets

Always choose the larger size rather than the smaller—you can cook a small fish in a large pan, but not vice versa. When buying, check to make sure your pots are right for your stove (flat, as opposed to coiled, electric elements require ground bases on pans).

If you can afford to buy top quality color-coordinated cookware, by all means buy it. Fine cookware makes a handsome display hanging from hooks and racks on wall or ceiling. If you must economize, remember that a few fine pans will last a lifetime and that the ability to use available equipment is one of the marks of a good cook.

Although all the pans illustrated above are not essential, you will find them helpful for cooking Grand Diplôme recipes, especially the following:
Stock pot or kettle: large, deep and heavy pan, about 8–10 quart capacity, for making and saving stock.
Double boiler: for cooking delicate sauces that burn easily.
Steamer: the perforated top portion holds vegetables, etc. for steaming.
Lasagne dish: shaped like a roasting pan, but suitable for serving at the table.

TYPES AND FINISHES

The following notes will give you some information about different metals; how to care for them, and how they'll affect your cooking.

Aluminum

Aluminum is a good conductor of heat, which makes for even cooking. This metal is durable and inexpensive too, but pots and pans of uncoated aluminum may pit and discolor if food is left in them for any length of time. If using an electric stove, check that the base of the pan is the right gauge. Some cast aluminum pans have an enamel or porcelainized finish; this removes the cleaning problems but the finish can chip.

Cast iron

Cast iron conducts heat slowly but evenly; for this reason it remains the classic choice of good cooks. Very handsome porcelainized cast iron is meant to be brought to the table, and the slick, colored finish makes the cookware easy to clean.

Without the porcelainized finish, cast iron must be oiled lightly after cleaning to prevent rusting and, unlike aluminum, it will break if dropped on a hard floor.

Copper

Copper conducts heat admirably, but it must be kept scrupulously clean. Every copper pan must have a thick lining of tin or nickel, otherwise poisonous salts will form in combination with certain foods.

Plain or enameled iron or steel

Both plain iron and plain steel may rust and they are not as good conductors of heat as aluminum. Enamel-coated iron is heavier and more durable than enamel-coated steel. The porcelain enamel coating most often used on these metals is very easy to clean.

Stainless steel

The easy cleaning qualities of stainless steel make it a popular choice, in spite of the fact that it is not a good conductor of heat. Many manufacturers compensate for this failing, either by producing cookware with copper or aluminum bottoms, or by making the bases of the pans 'three-ply' with an inner core of either copper or aluminum.

Other types of ovenware: glass and glass ceramic; porcelain; earthenware; stoneware

Generally speaking, all these are poor heat conductors but good heat retainers. Never subject any of them to sudden temperature changes – unless specially treated, they will tend to break or crack if suddenly filled with boiling fluid. Some porcelain and glassware utensils can be used over direct heat if you are careful, but be sure they are marked 'flameproof'. Glass ceramic ovenware marketed under trade names such as Pyrex and Corning, is both inexpensive and often attractive enough to take to the table. It heats slowly so a little extra time must be allowed in some recipes. Once hot, it retains heat well and needs a lower flame than metal pans.

Flameproof

This means that a utensil can withstand a direct flame on top of a stove. Some flame-proof pots and pans, however, must be used with wire supports and are not suitable for use on electric stoves, so check on this point when you buy. Flameproof utensils are usually poor conductors of heat, but are easy to clean.

Ovenproof or heatproof

Ovenproof or heatproof utensils cannot be placed *over* direct heat. They should not be transferred directly from oven or grill to a wood or plastic surface, or to the sink, but to a heat-resistant trivet or mat until they cool.

Non-stick finish

This finish isn't perfect, but it does ensure that food won't stick (which is particularly useful in a milk saucepan and some sauté pans). The interior plastic coating does not affect the heat-conducting properties of the metal to which it is applied.

HOW TO CLEAN YOUR POTS AND PANS

Good pots and pans deserve only the best treatment. If you take care of them when new, they will stand up better during long, hard wear. A pan that is seasoned (the surface thoroughly impregnated with oil so food does not stick), is much less likely to scorch foods and will improve with use.

If a pan is badly burned, let it cool a little, then fill it with water and some liquid detergent, place over moderate heat and boil until the encrusted food comes loose. Never add water to a burned pan that is very hot; the sudden cold will warp metal and crack porcelain or glass.

However, once a pan has been badly burned, it will always have a tendency to scorch, no matter how thoroughly it has been cleaned.

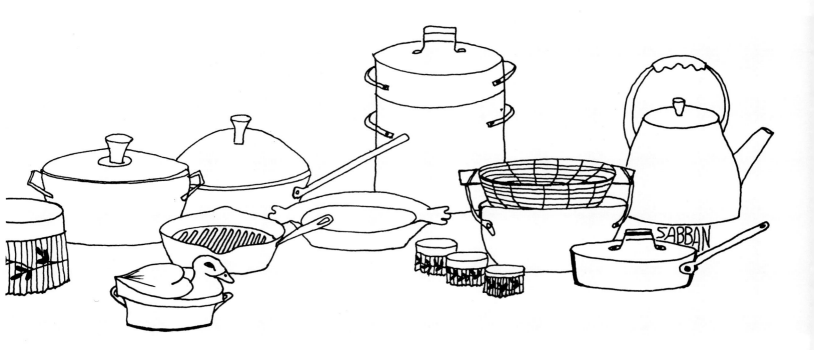

The following notes will help you clean your different types of pots and pans.

Aluminum

Do not soak aluminum because some water contains alkaline chemicals that will darken and stain the pot.

To remove stains, simmer an acid mixture like tomato juice, or water and vinegar, in the pot or add 1–2 tablespoons of cream of tartar to 1 quart of water and boil 10 minutes. Then scour with a soap-filled steel wool pad.

Cast iron

Cast iron pots should always be seasoned when purchased. First wash with detergent and water. Then coat inside with an unsalted liquid vegetable oil or shortening. Put the pot in a low oven (300°F) and leave for several hours. Remove the pan occasionally and distribute the oil by rubbing with a paper towel.

If a pan has been seasoned successfully, it will not rust. Do not use detergents for cleaning — only soap and water. Scour if necessary with a soap-filled steel wool pad, dry quickly over high heat, then rub with paper towels.

All cast iron pots should be stored without the lid to prevent moisture from building up inside the pan and causing rust.

Stainless steel

Household cleansers and detergents are effective if the stainless steel is not severely discolored. For a stainless steel pot with a bottom layer of aluminum, clean with a soap-filled steel wool pad.

For a stainless steel pot with a bottom layer of copper, clean the copper base with the cut edge of a lemon rubbed with salt, or with a commercial copper cleanser.

Porcelain enamel

Remove hard-water films by boiling a solution of vinegar and water in the pot.

Copper

Clean with a mixture of lemon juice, or vinegar, with salt. If badly stained, clean first with a soap-filled steel wool pad and then apply a coat of copper cleanser. Some copper pots are coated with a layer of lacquer when purchased. This can be removed with a thinner such as acetone, or as suggested on the pan label.

Glass

Clean glass pots with a household cleanser or a solution of baking soda and water to remove discoloration. Do not use a coarse cleanser that might scratch the surface. Clean glass ceramic with a household cleaner or stainless steel cleaner, or with drops of ammonia.

Non-stick finishes

Initially, the pot should be seasoned by wiping with oil. If grease builds up, remove by boiling a mixture of 2 tablespoons baking soda or $\frac{1}{2}$ cup of liquid chlorine bleach per cup of water, or use a special non-stick coating cleanser.

Afterwards, reseason. For normal washing, clean with soapy water and a soft cloth or a plastic mesh scourer.

Before buying a refrigerator for the first time, or replacing your present one, consider the following points:

1. Will the overall dimensions fit your kitchen?
2. Do you need a right- or a left-hand hinged door?
3. Does the volume (cubic feet) give you suitable shelf space (square feet) for your kind of food?
4. Do you want an automatic ice-maker?
5. Is the frozen food compartment large enough? Does it have a separate door?
6. Does the model have automatic or push-button defrost?
7. Are the shelves flexible enough for your requirements?
8. Check the guarantee — are costs of labor, spare parts, and carrying charges included?
9. Does the door open within the overall width?
10. Is the door handle flush to avoid accidental bumping?
11. Is the door seal magnetic to ensure tight closing?
12. Are fittings of durable metal rather than plastic?
13. Are shelves firm but easy to move? Do they lock to avoid sliding out completely?
14. Is there a charge for delivery and installation?

Modern refrigerators have come a long way from the cumbersome wooden cabinets used around the beginning of the 19th century. The illustration below shows some of the early cabinet ice boxes of that period; they were made of grained and varnished oak, lined with zinc, and were of ''the best quality procurable''.

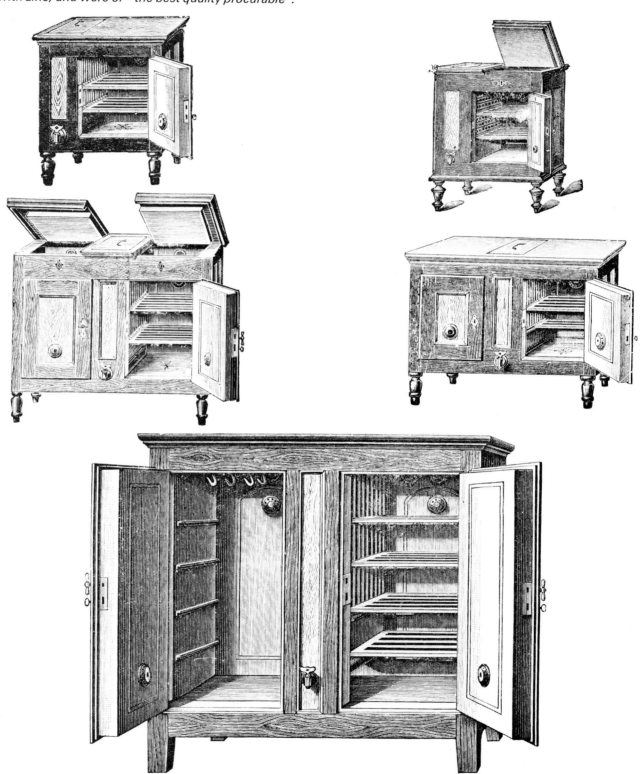

About Your Refrigerator

A refrigerator does a big job in your kitchen.

It's a storehouse for salad vegetables meant to be served crisp and cold; it speeds up many processes such as setting gelatin; it helps you to prepare hours ahead; and it keeps food in splendid condition so that shopping for specials can save both time and money.

Not only does it keep food cold, but it offers a choice of temperatures ranging from cool to cold to freezing and frequently to below freezing. These gradations are extremely important to good cooks and good cooking.

In a properly designed refrigerator, the circulating air gathers moisture from food over which it passes and, as it passes over the cold zone, it deposits some of this moisture as frost on the cooling unit. This is one of the reasons why hot food should not be put in the refrigerator — there will be too rapid a buildup of frost.

The two general groups of refrigerators are the **standard** or **conventional** models and the **refrigerator-freezers** or **combinations**.

The **standard** models have fresh food storage and a limited amount of space for short term preservation of frozen food. This type of refrigerator has a single exterior door and, since it is opened frequently, temperature fluctuations in the freezer section are not conducive to long storage of frozen food. Generally these refrigerators are the lowest priced models in the manufacturer's line and their operating costs are less than those of the combination refrigerator-freezer. The fresh food section is always located below the frozen food compartment and it holds foods above freezing temperatures ranging from 37°F–45°F. The frozen food storage area has below freezing temperatures averaging 10°F–15°F, but this is not a true freezer and should not be used as such.

In the **combination refrigerator-freezer,** the two main compartments are sealed off from each other. The freezer section holds food at 0°F, thus allowing storage of frozen foods. Temperature in the fresh food compartment is often several degrees lower than in the standard models.

Whatever type of refrigerator you buy, get the largest one you can afford — from the standpoint of kitchen space and money. Look for good quality materials, good sound construction, easy-to-manipulate and easy-to-clean features. Metal meat trays and vegetable crispers, rather than plastic, are well worth the extra cost. They are easier to clean, will not break, and generally cool foods more quickly. In fact, any movable part of the refrigerator that is handled frequently, such as trays or sliding shelves, needs to be sturdy and free of sharp edges. All pullout shelves should have a positive-lock position to prevent them from sliding out. Look for shelves that can be shifted from one level to another. This convenience will be appreciated when there are tall bottles and large containers to be stored.

Since a refrigerator is used by the average family for about 15 years, consider the cost — adding extras and how much they will be worth to you over the years, e.g. swing-out shelves, separate butter and cheese compartments with temperature control, ice cube ejectors, automatic ice-making equipment — all these represent an additional outlay of cash, and are of varying importance to different people.

If kitchen space is scarce, it may be most convenient to buy a refrigerator that fits under a work surface, one that has its own work surface, or a model that hangs on the wall. Look for door construction that permits you to open the door without having to leave extra swing space at the corner. Test this by removing vegetable crispers and other large containers when the door is partially open. If the door has to be swung more than a right angle (90°), it will interfere with placing your refrigerator in a corner. A foot pedal is a convenience, particularly if you have limited counter space next to the door opening. Some door handles are more comfortable to reach and grasp than others.

Defrosting is a necessary chore with some refrigerators. When ice builds up on the coils, it cuts down the efficiency of the evaporator, making the unit work overtime. It is impossible to say categorically how often a refrigerator should be defrosted, but a layer of ice $\frac{1}{4}$ inch thick is about the limit.

Many refrigerators have a push-button defrosting device that operates a special circuit. The temperature in the refrigerator remains in the safety zone and when the defrosting is finished the refrigerator switches itself back on. Some models have an automatic defrosting device that may be started by a time switch, or by the number of times the door is opened or the thickness of the ice. This is a feature that is well worth having.

If you don't have a refrigerator with an automatic defroster, you will have to take the foods out of the frozen food storage compartment when defrosting. Otherwise, unless you are cleaning the refrigerator, there is no need to remove ordinary food.

Using a refrigerator

Food packages, bowls or whatever container the food is stored in should be placed on the shelves so there is good circulation of air; they should not be jammed together.

Food should be wrapped or covered with foil or plastic wrap to prevent it from drying out, or the transfer of flavor from one food to the other. With plastic wrap, where wrap is transparent, foods can be easily identified. With foil-wrapped foods, be sure to label the packages.

The chart (overleaf) applies only to food that is perfectly fresh; it suggests positions for different foods in the refrigerator and how long they may be kept. But it is impossible to give precise lengths of time for food storage; the best guide is 'if in doubt, throw it out'.

Note: the temperature of the different areas in your refrigerator will vary according to the model so consult the manufacturer's handbook. Freezers and the preparation of food for freezing will be discussed in a future Volume.

STORAGE CHART

FOOD	HOW TO STORE	KEEPS IN REFRIGERATOR
Milk		
Fresh	Original container, closed	3–4 days near coldest section
Sour cream, buttermilk	Original container, closed	10–14 days in door
Cream	Original container, closed	3–4 days near coldest section
Eggs		
Fresh in shell	In covered container or in rack with pointed end down	3 weeks, any section
Yolks	Covered with water, if unbroken; or with pinch of salt if broken	1–2 days in cold section
Whites, separated	Covered lightly	3–5 days in cold section
Hard-cooked in shell	Uncovered section	1 week in moderate
Cheese		
Hard	In plastic wrap or foil, or in airtight container	Depending on type: up to 3 months in least cold section
Soft or cream	As above	1 week, in moderate section; remove at least 2 hours before serving
Fats		
Butter, margarine, cooking fats	Original wrapper	1–2 weeks in moderate section. Hold only 1–2 days in butter keeper
Cooked meats		
Roasts, casseroles, sliced meats, ham, cold meats	Cover with foil, or put in plastic container, so surfaces cannot dry out	2–3 days in coldest section

Information from Home Service Department, Potomac Electric Power Co., Washington, D.C.

FOOD	HOW TO STORE	KEEPS IN REFRIGERATOR
Uncooked meats		
Roasts, chops, steaks	If prepackaged, loosen pack; if not, remove market wrapper and re-wrap in wax paper	3–5 days in coldest section
Stewing meats, ground meat, variety meat	As above	1–2 days in cold section
Sausages, sliced bacon	If prepackaged, leave in pack; if not, wrap in wax paper or put in a plastic container	7–10 days in cold section
Fresh Fish and Shellfish	Remove market paper, re-wrap in wax paper or plastic bag, sealing to avoid odor leakage	1 day in coldest section
Cooked dishes	As for cooked meats	2–3 days in coldest section
Poultry		
Fresh whole	If prepackaged, loosen pack; if not, wipe and wrap in plastic wrap or wax paper	2–3 days in cool section
Cooked	Remove stuffing. When cool, wrap or cover as for cooked meats above	2–3 days in cool section
Cooked dishes	Cover with lid, plastic wrap or foil. Refrigerate when cool	1 day in cool section
Fruit and Vegetables		
Soft fruits—strawberries, raspberries, etc.	Remove any rotten fruit. Do not wash. Store in covered container or uncovered in vegetable drawer	2–3 days in moderate section
Oranges, lemons	Store in vegetable drawer	7–10 days
Salad vegetables	Clean and drain, store in plastic container or wrap in plastic wrap or uncovered in vegetable drawer	3–5 days

MEASURING & MEASUREMENTS

The recipe quantities in the Course are measured in standard level teaspoons, tablespoons and cups and their equivalents are shown below. Any liquid pints and quarts also refer to U.S. standard measures.

When measuring dry ingredients, fill the cup or spoon to overflowing without packing down and level the top with a knife. All the dry ingredients, including flour, should be measured before sifting, although sifting may be called for later in the instructions.

Butter and margarine usually come in measured sticks (1 stick equals $\frac{1}{2}$ cup) and other bulk fats can be measured by displacement. For $\frac{1}{3}$ cup fat, fill the measuring cup $\frac{2}{3}$ full of water. Add fat until the water reaches the 1 cup mark. Drain the cup of water and the fat remaining equals $\frac{1}{3}$ cup.

For liquids, fill the measure to the brim, or to the calibration line.

Often quantities of seasonings cannot be stated exactly, for ingredients vary in the amount they require. The instructions 'add to taste' are literal, for it is impossible to achieve just the right balance of flavors in many dishes without tasting them.

Liquid measure	Volume equivalent
3 teaspoons	1 tablespoon
2 tablespoons	1 fluid oz
4 tablespoons	$\frac{1}{4}$ cup
16 tablespoons	1 cup or 8 fluid oz
2 cups	1 pint
2 pints	1 quart
4 quarts	1 gallon

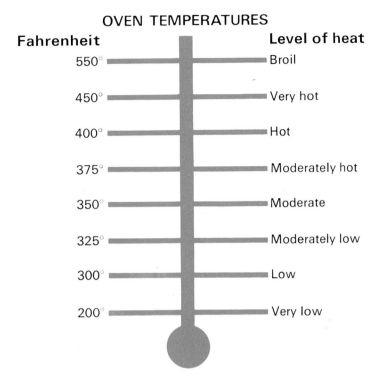

OVEN TEMPERATURES

Fahrenheit		Level of heat
550°		Broil
450°		Very hot
400°		Hot
375°		Moderately hot
350°		Moderate
325°		Moderately low
300°		Low
200°		Very low

OVEN TEMPERATURES AND SHELF POSITIONS

Throughout the Cooking Course, oven temperatures are stated in degrees Fahrenheit and in generally agreed levels of heat such as 'high' and 'moderate'. The equivalents are shown on the table above.

However, exact temperature varies in different parts of an oven and the thermostat reading refers to the heat in the middle. As the oven temperature at top and bottom can vary as much as 25°F from this setting, the positioning of shelves is very important. In general, heat rises, so the hottest part of the oven is at the top, but consult the manufacturer's handbook about your individual model.

Pans and dishes of food should be placed parallel with burners or elements to avoid scorched edges.

When baking cakes, there must be room for the heat to circulate in the oven around baking sheets and cake pans; otherwise the underside of the cakes will burn. If baking more than one cake in an oven that has back burners or elements, arrange the cakes side by side. If the oven has side burners, arrange cakes back and front.

Oven thermostats are often inaccurate and are unreliable at extremely high or low temperatures. If you do a great deal of baking or question the accuracy of your oven, use a separate oven thermometer as a check on the thermostat.

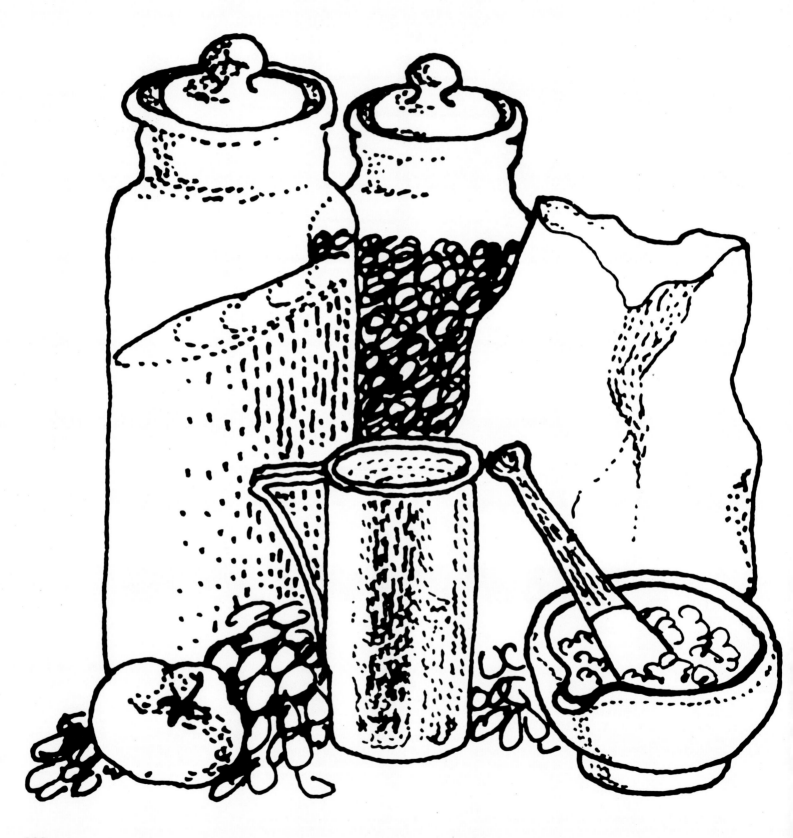

INDEX

(Volumes 1 & 2)

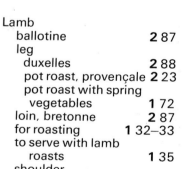

MN

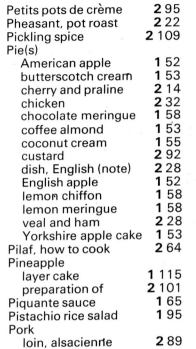

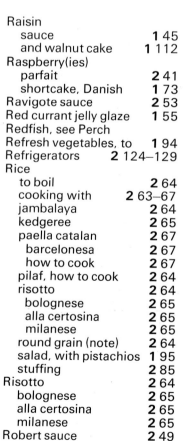

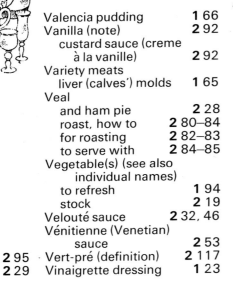

Acknowledgments

Photographs by Fred J. Maroon: pages 25, 37, 56, 66, 67, 105. Other photographs by Michael Leale, Roger Phillips, John Cowderoy, Peter Lloyd, David Cripps and John Ledger. Photograph on page 55 courtesy of Brown & Polson. Coffee and Coffee Pots by Tina Laver. Pots and Pans by Diana McLellan.

COOKING CURIOSITIES

Soyer's Miniature Kitchen

Alexis Soyer was not only one of the leading chefs of the 19th century but also one of the most inventive.

While he was chef at the Reform Club in London, England, he designed a compact kitchen for the S.S. Guadalquiver. The illustration below shows the interior of the ship's kitchen, and the figures are a key to its layout. His design combined economy of space with the most methodical arrangement in the small space of 8 feet wide X 17 feet long.

So well arranged was the kitchen that dinner for 100 people was easily prepared.

Notes

Notes

Notes